C000148974

Andy Bull was born in 195[   ]
up in Kent. He has a degree [   ]
from the University of Lanc[   ]
since 1977, on the *Daily Mail* and the *Independent*, and is
now Features Editor on the *Mail on Sunday*. His travel
writing has won him a commendation in the British
Press Awards. He is married, has two young children
and lives in Ealing, west London. Andy Bull's book
Coast to Coast, which explores the pop landscape of
America, is also available in Black Swan.

Strange Angels

Andy Bull

BLACK SWAN

For Beatrice

STRANGE ANGELS
A BLACK SWAN BOOK : 0 552 99572 X

First publication in Great Britain

PRINTING HISTORY
Black Swan edition published 1995

Set in 11/12pt Linotype Melior by
Phoenix Typesetting, Ilkley, West Yorkshire

Black Swan Books are published by Transworld Publishers Ltd,
61-63 Uxbridge Road, London W5 5SA,
in Australia by Transworld Publishers (Australia) Pty Ltd,
15-25 Helles Avenue, Moorebank, NSW 2170
and in New Zealand by Transworld Publishers (NZ) Ltd,
3 William Pickering Drive, Albany, Auckland.

Reproduced, printed and bound in Great Britain by
Cox & Wyman Ltd, Reading, Berks.

Acknowledgements

I am indebted to everyone who allowed me to tell their stories in this book, those who would not, and others who opened doors and put me on the right track. On a few occasions I have honoured requests not to include full names in the text. My particular thanks go to Linda Kay, Roman Hryniszak, Michelle Grimes, Dennis Smith, David Loehr, Sylvia Bongiovanni, Yugi Mitani, Mark Holland, Cyndi Silvia, Nancy Johnson, Dr George Arndt, and the staff and pupils of the St Marylebone School, London.

My especial thanks go to Elaine Newcombe for her invaluable assistance with research.

Contents

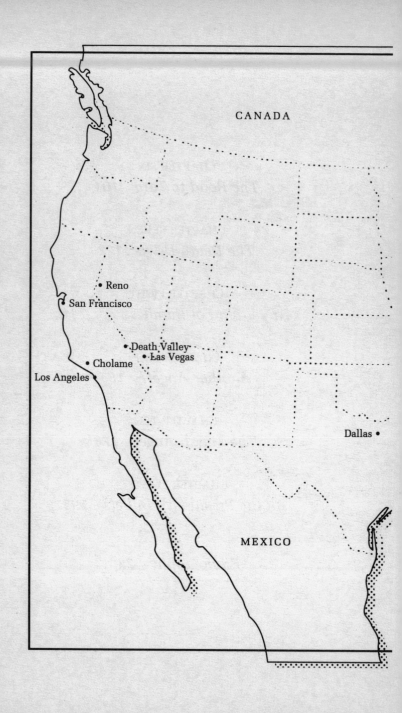

Plainfield •

New York •

• Fairmount

Washington •

• Memphis

• Atlanta

Jonesboro •

THE GULF OF MEXICO

When people stop believing in God they don't
believe in nothing; they believe in anything.

G. K. Chesterton

Introduction

Between Buckingham Palace and Death Valley I got the big picture.

But it was the Throne Room that first set me thinking.

It was the day before the Queen threw the palace doors open to the world's great, rubbernecking unwashed. Today was Press day, a crush of wide-eyed foreign correspondents gushing and gasping about the grace and splendour of it all, art critics muttering to each other about a hideousness beyond their powers of description, and sniggering general hacks just wishing that they had an anti-royalist proprietor who would allow them to take the piss in print.

Certainly the palace was an assault on the senses, a mixture of the richly ornate and the threadbare and outmoded. There was a Milky Bar and Liquorice Allsort Grand Staircase inspired by Hansel and Gretel's house, the bilious nightmare of the Green Drawing Room, and a 55-ft-long Picture Gallery with a glass roof like a Victorian railway station. It was heated with grand, colonnaded, two-bar electric fires that Mussolini would have loved.

The only spot of humour came in the White Drawing Room – very Barry Manilow, very flattering to a mahogany tan – where at the press of a button the Royals can suddenly materialize before their startled guests. The mirror to the left of the fireplace swings open and the Queen and her family step out of their hiding place in the Royal Closet. Beam me up Your Royal Highness.

The palace was a jangle of screaming crimsons, golds and Prussian blues, a jumble of furniture from several centuries and many styles. Truly a dog's breakfast.

And that Throne Room.

In the Throne Room it occurred to me that if Elvis Presley had had a palace to work on instead of just a relatively modest pile of stones on a hill south of Memphis, he could have created this – except that he would have made a better job of it.

And if the British Royal family, who easily match Elvis in tastelessness, had also had something of his bloated imagination, they might have put together a pile that was worth seeing.

If only they had asked his advice about the Throne Room, with acres of swirling mulberry-juice carpet that the great and the good down the centuries have had to cross on their way to a gong, and drapes that make every window look like a Punch and Judy booth. Yes, it had its vast crystal chandeliers, but it was still underwhelming in its impact. Very 1950s Odeon, very *palais de danse*.

The greatest disappointment was that it did not even have a throne. So how can they call it a throne room? Elvis would have had a throne. Twin, his and hers thrones in gold, covered in rhinestones, with nooks for Thirstbusters of Coke in the armrests and a control panel that would bring a bank of TVs down from the ceiling.

All the Queen had been able to come up with were two red chairs, relics of the 1953 Coronation. Embroidered in gold on their backrests were the initials ER and P – the Royal equivalent of the Wayne and Tracey that used to appear on the sun-strips of Cortinas.

The Throne Room revealed much about the Royal family's fusty, moth-eaten decline. Now that the Princess of Wales, whose Essex-girl glamour had put them on the front pages of every magazine in the world,

14

had broken off diplomatic relations, what were they left with? The Throne Room said it all.

A hidden door in the corner of the room, disguised with the same silk that covered the walls, had a sign reading Emergency Exit on it and a picture of a man running.

I was that man running.

Running on empty. Victim of my own personal decline. Stuck in a job with a newspaper that was crumbling. For seven years I had worked at the *Independent*, which was launched in 1986 and became an essential yuppie accessory, until its proprietors foolishly destroyed the financial viability of the company by launching a Sunday newspaper just as the deepest recession since the 1930s was about to bite. Now it was haemorrhaging cash and waiting for a takeover. I had been looking for the courage to quit and what hit me in the Throne Room made me do so.

What hit me was a thought about heroes. Standing in the Queen's palace I had been thinking of Elvis Presley. Millions of people think about Elvis Presley still. Unlike the Royal family, which is Britain's only real claim to a world-class act, he is not in decline. But then, he is not still alive. He can't do anything to damage his image.

Nor is Marilyn Monroe alive. Or James Dean or, for that matter, John F. Kennedy.

And yet these four are among the most famous people in the world, arguably even more famous now than they were when they were alive.

It just goes to show: if you want to live for ever, die young.

I know these people are alive (truly alive – never mind whether they are breathing or not) because I hear so much about them. I see them everywhere; I read about them, watch them.

Marilyn's blond, pouting image is reproduced endlessly as the ideal embodiment of feminine sexuality.

James Dean is still the ultimate teenage rebel, with an

image so potent it can sell anything – savings accounts to British students, blank video tapes to the Japanese and Gap khaki trousers to the world.

Elvis's resurrection is such a fervent wish of many people that sightings of him are commonplace. Women move to Memphis to dedicate their lives to this dead singer. Some believe he is a Christ figure, others merely want to carry on his good works.

Hundreds of people flock every day to Dealey Plaza in Dallas, where Kennedy was shot, to try and decide for themselves whether Lee Harvey Oswald could have acted as a lone assassin. Regularly there are new books, films, documentaries – and theories, theories, theories.

So, standing in the Throne Room, I asked myself why it is that our greatest living heroes have been dead for fifteen, thirty, thirty-five years or more?

I didn't know the answer, but I decided to find it. I was going to discover why the world is obsessed with these characters, why they are icons, role models, fantasy figures; why for some they are gods – angels.

What strange angels they make!

Marilyn was a neurotic, self-destructive orphan, Elvis a fat, drugged-out singer, Kennedy a compulsive womanizer, Dean an awkward, sulky farm boy.

They were cracked, confused individuals, the most unlikely objects for sustained adulation. And yet they have grown to embody the very essence of the American dream: the power of an individual through personality, sheer talent, willpower and irresistible charisma to perform the modern miracle and become world-famous.

Long after their deaths, this quartet have hundreds of thousands, millions of dedicated fans. The most ardent of those fans follow their idols, creating unique rituals around them, marking their birthdays and death days, turning the places where they were born, lived and died into shrines.

So I quit, and got on a plane for America. I sat with my USA road atlas and began to draw up an itinerary that would take in the significant places associated with these people on their significant dates.

When I had established that Marilyn died in Los Angeles on 5 August, that Elvis died in Memphis on 16 August, that James Dean died in the desert north of L.A. on 30 September, and that JFK died in Dallas on 22 November, things began to fall into place.

I was working out a trip across America which would lock me into a tour of dead heroes in the company, I hoped, of the most excessive dead-hero worshippers I could find. For I do have one confession to make. In the same way that upright Victorian families would pop along to their local asylum on a Sunday afternoon to be entertained by the antics of the insane, I like to travel America and get close to a succession of obsessives. I wanted crazies to fill these pages.

And I was to meet some wonders. There would be Michelle, who believes absolutely that Marilyn Monroe's soul entered her body shortly after the star's death. On the James Dean Death Drive – in which fans follow his final journey from Los Angeles to the spot 150 miles away in the desert close to Paso Robles where his Porsche Spider was fatally struck by a Ford – I would meet Ralph. Ralph is one of the dozens of conspiracy theorists, vintage-car buffs and James Dean lookalikes who, on the anniversary of his death, like to stand on the very spot at which Dean died at the very same time of day, so that they see the world exactly as Jimmy last saw it.

And I would meet Dan, who believes he is the only man who knows the truth about JFK, and who stands for six days a week, fifty-two weeks of the year, at Dealey Plaza, telling anyone who will listen about his theory.

It wasn't just the characters, but the places too. If you want to understand people and what they made of themselves, your best bet is to go to the places they were from, the places which made them. I was to learn a great deal about James Dean in the archetypal

American small town of Fairmount, Indiana where he grew up. His secret was right there.

But first I had to clear my head of England and all I had left behind. I needed mountain air to do that. And as I studied my map of California I noticed, far off in the empty outback, behind the lush coastal strip on which the cities and the people were crammed, a spot marked 'Highest point in contiguous USA'. It was Mount Whitney, elevation 14,494 feet and shaded a deep green. And then I noticed, four inches or 148 miles away, another point marked, this time on a deep brown background, 'Lowest point in USA'. This was Badwater, at minus 283 feet.

To go from the highest point to the lowest, from cool heaven to blazing hell in a matter of hours, was so appealing that I had to do it. And so, the morning after next, I awoke in a Garden of Eden on the shores of Mirror Lake, high on the eastern slopes of Mount Whitney, in an alpine meadow covered in wild flowers.

I had hiked up the previous afternoon, complete with hired tent, permit and much sage advice from a ranger about how to hang my food from a tree to keep it away from bears. At dawn I awoke to a day so clear I wanted to turn the brightness down, the white and grey peaks reflected perfectly in the still lake, and set out on a ten-mile hike along the rocky path through the pines to the road where I had had to abandon my car.

As I walked I reflected that I could not distance myself from the strange angels I was pursuing. I was in their thrall too, intrigued to find out more about them. I can still remember the diary entry I made, aged seven, on the day I learned that Kennedy had been shot dead. It was accompanied by a drawing of a man in a long black car, with another man standing on top of a tall brown building, holding a gun. From the muzzle of the gun a dotted pencil line ran down to the head of the man in the car.

All those who go to Dealey Plaza, who peer from the window in the book depository from which Lee Harvey Oswald is supposed to have murdered the President, do so because they want to see for themselves, to make up their own minds, whether Oswald could have done it, or whether they have been lied to for thirty years. Had I, as a seven-year-old boy, been lied to?

And those others, Elvis and Marilyn and Jimmy Dean. I can vividly remember the electric thrill of first hearing 'Heartbreak Hotel', of being entranced by the luminous presence of Marilyn in *The Misfits*, of seeing *Rebel Without A Cause* as a teenager and thinking, forget the unnatural colour, the mannered performances, the melodramatic plot, this man had an inner core, some kind of fire inside him that I was instantly drawn to and understood. He was me, as he was every teenager, and Marilyn was every woman you ever wanted.

So, as I came to the start of the road, picked up my car and took the switchback road down the flank of the Sierra Nevadas, as I looked across the dusty Salina Valley 10,000 feet below to the hazy Inyo Mountains, I decided that – what the hell – this would be a personal journey too. Because it was *The Misfits*, of all Marilyn's films, that captivated me, I would seek her in the desert around Reno, Nevada, where it was filmed.

And I would broaden my journey out, so that it covered not just the four great, all-time modern icons, but others who gripped my imagination, such as the fictional character of Scarlett O'Hara, heroine of Margaret Mitchell's novel and David O. Selznick's film *Gone with the Wind*. The book has sold 28,000,000 copies, making it the most popular novel ever written.

When plans to film the sequel were announced, 20,000 women auditioned. In Atlanta, where the book is set, Scarlett and Rhett Butler lookalikes abound. Visitors come from as far afield as Japan and Europe in search of Tara, Scarlett's plantation home. For thousands of people, Scarlett O'Hara is as alive as my long-dead quartet – and she never existed in the first place. How could a fictional character hold such sway? Jonesboro, the little town south of Atlanta in which the story is set, went on my itinerary.

And as I dropped through the brown, baked earth of the Alabama Hills which Hollywood once colonized and where the roads and canyons are named after the films and TV shows that were created there, I decided to take in another character. Although few have ever heard of him, he has exercised a terrifying and abiding pull on our imaginations through two compelling films made thirty years apart. This man was Ed Gein, the real-life murderer who inspired Alfred Hitchcock's *Psycho* and Thomas Harris's *Silence of the Lambs*. What fascinated me was that what he did, in a small town called Plainfield in icy Wisconsin, was so awful that both films toned down his savagery. Despite it all, his truth was still stranger than either fiction. Who knew anything about him? Anyone who watched those films knows a great deal more than they might imagine.

I took a turn down Movie Road to Lone Ranger Canyon, saw the spot where Roy Rogers found Trigger, where *Bonanza* was filmed, and the *Gunga Din* village where that 1939 film of the Brits in India was made. John Wayne had ridden these hills countless times, galloping along the passes between strangely shaped rocks to which locals had given names such as the Spooks, Elephant Rock, Batman, the Bishop and the Football Player.

From the one-tree town of Lone Pine, where the temperature was already 40 degrees Fahrenheit higher than at breakfast time, the road sped me over the empty, burnt-out valley, past the dry bed of Owens Lake, over the Inyo Mountains and the Panamint Range to the very lip of Death Valley itself.

The final descent from 5,000 feet to sea level took maybe ten minutes, and was like plunging head first into an inferno. Below me I could see the road, snaking like a rivulet of molten silver through the ash of the valley floor. The heat nipped at my ears in a way that only frost had before. In this dry heat I did not sweat, just felt like my extremities might blacken, shrivel and fall off. As I descended, the thermometer rose, so that it was 110°F when I pulled off the road at Stovepipe Wells, one of only two points of habitation on the valley floor.

As I picked up my pen to write it bent under the pressure of my fingers and hot black ink oozed out. A couple of scraggy black birds swiftly picked the dead bugs from my radiator grille. The water in the drinking fountain at the general store was too hot to sip, so I went inside and bought a bottle called Crystal Geyser. The label told me it had – like me – begun its current journey on a peak of Mount Whitney, had filtered through the rock to emerge at a spring at 4,000 feet. From there it had been bottled, and paralleled the rest of my journey down to the very floor of Death Valley. And then I drank it. Fate, I guess.

Once this place instilled terror into the traveller. For the early settlers, trekking west to California's Promised Land, it was a place of threat, to be traversed with trepidation. Look at the names they gave its prominent features: Dante's View, Coffin Peak, Hell's Gate.

Today the traveller could cruise across the valley in his air-conditioned car, maybe step out briefly here at Stovepipe Wells, founded in 1926 as Bungalette City in the first attempt to cater for the tourist, then jump back into the cool of the automobile and rush on to the luxury desert-resort hotel twenty miles away at Furnace Creek.

But Death Valley still has the power to inspire and amaze. It is a land of illusion. To my left as I moved on were sand dunes of perfect, silky whiteness, sculpted by the wind. Beyond were rocky foothills like uncut diamonds. I stopped the car and walked towards a

21

lake which I expected to discover was a mirage at any moment. Underfoot was not sand but a hard dry substance which resembled concrete mix awaiting water. There were occasional tufts of grass so dry they turned to dust when trodden on, and bushes of miniature white holly, its translucent leaves lit pink by the sun.

The lake proved not to be a mirage but a bed of dully glowing salt and minerals, a puffy white crust on the oozing mud. It powdered in my hand. I touched the tip of my tongue to it and tasted first salt, and then other, alien mineral flavours which made me spit hurriedly.

I took a few steps over the salt and found that there was actually water of a kind beneath the crust – but of such a thick, sluggish consistency that it would be useless to even the most desperately thirsty traveller. It was like walking on the moon, or tramping through a surreal land from the mind of Dali. I half expected to find soft clocks melting in the sun. There was further weirdness to come as I drove on, past the Devil's Golf Course where huge salt nodules have solidified into lava that is shaped like the bunkers you might find on a post-nuclear holocaust St Andrews.

At the Furnace Creek Inn I stopped off for a cold beer, marvelling at how man can so easily turn nature on its head and make this hell a place of casual pleasures. There were just me and the barman in the bar – the kind of instinctive analyst who wheedles your life story out of you with a couple of simple questions then wanders off, leaving you burbling into your beer. So of course I told him about my journey, and he told me a story about Marilyn Monroe.

'Marilyn has been here,' he said. 'Long time ago, when she was very young, brought by an army photographer named David Conover. This was long before she made it in the movies. It was wartime and Conover was out to shoot pictures of pretty girls for a cheesecake magazine for the troops. He has claimed he slept with her here. I don't know whether he did or not but it's a nice romantic little story. I guess it was just a sixteen-room motel when Marilyn was here, not a desert resort like it is now. Guess who Conover's commanding officer was?'

I could not.

'Ronald Reagan. Coincidence, huh?'

And the story got me thinking about the angels again. How just about anybody you met could casually dredge up a little tale about them. Nostalgia accounted for part of their appeal. Marilyn, Dean, Elvis and JFK came from a simpler time, from the fifties and sixties when America was at its zenith. They were symbols of that, of an America which was optimistic, affluent, idealistic. There were things to believe in then: the race to the moon, the principles of a politician.

The seamy side was kept hidden when these people were alive: Kennedy's womanizing, Marilyn's suicidal tendencies, Elvis's bloated, drug-addicted state. They came from America's finest hour, they were at the pinnacle of a popular culture that the world loved, that it still loves and wants to be a part of. They were able to die with their ideal unsullied. It was only after their death that the image was attacked, and by then it was too late. Whatever we know of them now, we revere them for what we thought of them then.

Kennedy was seen as the archetypal leader, the clean-cut, idealistic charmer. His obsession with sex was not generally known. James Dean is portrayed as a masochistic, promiscuous homosexual in one of his latest biographies. But so what? If such stories were proved, the fans would not believe them. James Dean's most devout followers don't even see him as a rebel, but rather as the typical well-scrubbed American boy next door. Why, he wouldn't even break the speed limit.

There will never be heroes like them again. How could any current star achieve such heights of posthumous adulation and reverence today, when heroes are destroyed during their lifetimes? Modern biography does not set out to celebrate a genius of whatever manifestation. It is not founded on our historic or psychological curiosity. Rather, it seeks to discover that the subject of any life story is actually no bigger or better than ourselves. Worse, if possible: more corrupt, more evil, less happy, less well-balanced.

There is no mystery to the modern superstar. Take Madonna, who bases her appeal and her persona on a mixture of reference to, and rejection of, the image of Marilyn the blonde bombshell. Marilyn was full of sexual promise that she never delivered. Madonna, conversely, will show you everything, as she frequently does in videos and books such as *Sex*, where she casts herself in every graphic sexual fantasy a fan could wish for.

And if the famous are different today, so are the fans. Formerly fans were devoted. They wanted to get close, to touch if they could, but there was no threat in their attentions. Today we have the phenomenon of the stalker. From tennis stars and minor royals to actresses and weathergirls, dozens of celebrities have been hounded by fans whose interest becomes a sick obsession, in which they may believe that the star/victim is secretly encouraging them, telling them they are desperately wanted.

In the space of a couple of weeks I counted cases in which the Channel Four newsreader Zeinab Badawi had to take action in court against a fan who believed Martians had ordered him to marry her, in which a TV presenter called Michaela Strachan received 3,000 letters from a crank, where an obsessed TV cameraman killed himself after Lady Helen Windsor married someone else and where a man who believed Ulrika Jonsson was sending him love messages via the telephone was found dead on a railway line.

But the fans of the long-dead icons who interest me want someone they can idolize still. And for that they need someone who cannot tarnish their image by misbehaviour or failure, who cannot be denigrated.

Because they are dead they enjoy an idealized existence in an idealized place: the past.

Six months after America marked the thirtieth anniversary of John F. Kennedy's assassination, the true nature of our adoration of heroes such as he was shown in the reaction to the death of his wife, Jacqueline Kennedy Onassis. It was to Kennedy and the golden years of his presidency that the obituarists and commentators harked back. Jackie was seen as the pristine survivor of the Kennedy legend, which the rest of the family has tarnished in the years since 1963. While other reputations waxed and waned, Jackie's remained inviolable. She was described as a princess and an icon.

Jacqueline Kennedy Onassis is seen in this ideal light still partly because, in a time when the star-maker machinery will chew up, swallow and spit out celebrity, she was the last great private public figure in America. In a time of gilt and glitz and perpetual revelation she was consistently private, dignified, distant.

When she died, people cried for a vanished concept of grace, style and class. But perhaps the most over-whelming response was one of nostalgia. Jackie was the last vestige of a charmed life. Those old enough to remember feel they were once a part of it. Those who are too young for that can feel a part of it through the way they revere her and John Kennedy. Visiting Dealey Plaza puts them in touch with a hero.

Another way to be associated with a star is to buy a relic. Someone paid £4,000 for the key to Marilyn Monroe's dressing room at 20th Century-Fox and £6,000 for a pair of her sequined opera-length gloves. Elvis Presley's American Express card made £27,500 and a two-inch square of carpet from his bedroom sold for £200. Even a photocopy of a job application made by Elvis in 1952 went for £800.

It is this desire to see or possess something which belonged to a star that feeds the round of fans' events.

From the tens of thousands who go to Graceland to shuffle round Elvis's grave site on the anniversary of his death on 16 August and who will take a leaf from one of his trees and a blade of grass from his lawn if they can, to the Japanese women who desperately want to find the actual house in which the fictional Scarlett O'Hara lived, they are trying to make a hero more real to them.

And while Scarlett O'Hara fans make a huge effort of will, seeking to force a fictional character into an existence in the real world, our fiction is often inspired by dead stars. John F. Kennedy appeared as a character in Don DeLillo's *Libra* and D. M. Thomas's *Flying Into Love*. Marilyn Monroe is a central character in *The Immortals* by Budd Schulberg, and in Bill Morris's *Biography of a Buick*, along with Elvis Presley.

Those who have known these icons become famous because of their association with them – however tenuous. The innocent bystanders at Kennedy's assassination have earned nicknames based on their descriptions – the Babushka Lady, the Deaf Mute, the Lady in Red. Several have written books giving their accounts of the six seconds it took to murder the President. When they appear at conventions for Kennedy conspiracy theorists they get a rapturous reception. They are heroes too.

Sitting in the bar at the Furnace Creek Inn I leafed through one of the fan magazines I had picked up earlier in Los Angeles. It was dedicated to Marilyn Monroe and was the newsletter of a fan club called, accurately enough, All About Marilyn. In it was an interview with James Haspiel, who as a teenager had followed Marilyn just about everywhere she went and became a friend of hers. Haspiel said: 'You can't sit down with her, you can't have a cup of coffee with her . . . you can only do it in a way by doing it with those who did it . . . Do you know who I am? I am . . . every one of you who cannot relate to Arthur Miller, Joe DiMaggio (her husbands) or Darryl Zanuck (boss of

20th Century-Fox, which employed her) . . . I represent you. I did it for myself and in retrospect, I did it for you. You can live it through me now!'

Haspiel also tackled another question that I had been pondering. Exactly what is it that fans are celebrating? Is it Marilyn Monroe, say, as a great actress, or Elvis as a wonderful singer?

I thought not. It seemed to me to go deeper than that. These people were revered not for their achievements or their narrow, professional abilities. Their appeal was much more fundamental, it had far more to do with what they were like, what they stood for, their personal essence.

Haspiel said this about Marilyn: 'We live in a society that celebrates great architecture, great music, sculpture . . . and nobody seems to get the reality that there is also human art. Marilyn was human art . . . that's exactly what she was.'

That seemed reasonable. All those people who wish fervently that Elvis was not dead, that he would some day reappear . . . did they want him to come back so that he could make another *Christmas Album*, or a few more tacky movies? Surely not. It was the man himself they wanted.

And, thinking of Marilyn, it was not really her abilities as an actress which brought her her true fame. This is why no blonde woman with large breasts will ever succeed in being the new Marilyn. The fact that she was an actress is irrelevant, really. The movies were just the way she happened to come to our attention. It is not for her performances that she is remembered, but for what she was.

What was she then?

Norman Mailer said in his book, *Marilyn*, that she 'was every man's love affair with America'. The *Guardian* writer W. J. Weatherby called her 'that mischievous, vulnerable, beautiful blonde who haunts the American Dream.'

There are the obvious facts in her continuing appeal

that she was a beauty who died in her prime, a woman who fulfilled the American dream; a poor orphan who became a star through her own innate abilities, reaching the top of her profession and being intimate with leaders like Kennedy and heroes like the footballer Joe DiMaggio.

John Huston, who directed Marilyn in two films, has suggested that her magic came not from her acting, but from her ability to explore herself and extricate some personal essence that was special and different. In 1976 the novelist Larry McMurtry came up with a wonderful phrase to describe Marilyn and explain why she fascinates. He called her a major ghost. He wrote of her in the *Washington Post*: 'Her presence still haunts our national consciousness. She is right in there with our major ghosts: Hemingway, the Kennedy brothers – people who finished with American life before America had time to finish with them.'

W. J. Weatherby picked up on the phrase when writing in the *Guardian* in 1992, saying: 'There are still some who . . . put her down as a childish, dumb blonde. The same scoffers dismiss John Kennedy's effect on the America of his time as mere public relations . . . But such simplifications fail to account for the profound influence these major ghosts continue to have on us.'

I passed the afternoon with these reveries and a few cold beers. When I finally got back on the desert road it was late in the afternoon. And when I arrived at Badwater the sun was setting, staining the sky a polluted purple, yellow and brown. A sign 283 feet up on the rock-face above the car park at Badwater showed the sea level, and brought home just how far below the ocean I stood. There was complete silence as the sun sank behind Telescope Peak.

A coach from Scenic Hyway Tours of San Francisco was parked alongside Badwater Lake and a cluster of little stick figures had walked the 400 yards over the salty sand to the water's edge. As they crouched to dip their fingers in the mineral-suffused, blood-hot water I was tempted to yell out a warning to them: 'Hey fellas. I found out what's poisoned the water. Elvis is lying out there. He's dead and he's stinkin'. Musta had a whole heap a chemicals in him.'

CHAPTER ONE

Getting in a Marilyn Mood

MARILYN MONROE,
LOS ANGELES, 5 AUGUST

She was sitting on the concrete, arms clutched around
her knees, looking up at the little brass plaque which
read

Marilyn Monroe
1926 – 1962

and the conical vase beside it which held a single,
bright yellow flower. She was rocking slightly from
side to side and singing softly. I sat on a bench a few
yards behind her and listened, trying to make out the
song, if such it was.

She wore sunglasses, and heavy gold-hoop earrings.
Her skin was very pale and her lips very red and she
had long, peroxide blond, tightly curled hair drawn
back from her face and passed through a band. It fell
between her shoulder-blades, heavy, almost in ringlets.
It was like the wig on a Marilyn Monroe judge.

And she crooned on, like Marilyn singing in her
bath.

And I thought, great. This is the real thing. Paydirt
at the first attempt. A 22-carat Marilyn Monroe crazy-
woman at the grave on the eve of the anniversary of
Marilyn's last day alive.

Den had been right. Dennis Call-me-Den Smith had
known exactly what he was talking about. I'd got to
Los Angeles with little time to spare before 5 August,

Marilyn's anniversary, my only contact his name and number on a scrap of paper. Den was an English expat. A spiky-haired Essex boy with a neat blue star tattooed on his right earlobe – a relic, he told me, of his days as bass player in Levi and the Rockettes. Now married to an American who was a writer on *LA Law*, he was the owner of a 1959 Presidential Cadillac with which he undertook Marilyn Monroe tours.

Actually, Den told me, he was in television too, though he also acted as driver to Mick Hucknell of Simply Red when he happened to be in L.A. Ducking and weaving. Little bit of this, little bit of that.

Den offered to take me on his Marilyn Monroe tour in search of suitable obsessives. The tour was not exactly oversubscribed. There was just me and an English couple called Paul and Victoria who sat in the back of the Caddy with their camcorder, muttering into the microphone an abbreviated version of Den's commentary as we toured the Marilyn sites.

Den had assured me that the place to go was the grave. You always got lookalikes up there, he said. I arranged that if I struck lucky he would leave me there.

So I sat up front in this great beast of a car, a long white killer shark with a radiator grille like a double row of razor teeth and twin rocket fins at the back. 'They only made 535 of them,' Den told us. 'There are probably only 200 left in the world, 100 in running order and this is the only one in Southern Cal. It cost me $7,500 which was OK but I had to spend another $10,000 on it – new paint job, new interior – and another $10,000 on spares. These were exclusively made for the White House staff, the secret service would have had these. When President Kennedy had Marilyn picked up for one of their little meetings it would have been in one. Could even have been this car.'

Den was very proud of his Marilyn tour.

'When I come over to L.A. three years ago the first

thing I did was I went down Hollywood Boulevard – cos I live on Hollywood Boulevard – and I asked everybody about Marilyn Monroe. Where she lived, where she was buried. And no-one could tell me. Nobody could take me on a Marilyn tour. There wasn't one. I thought there's a space to be filled here, so I took it on.'

Out at Westwood Village Cemetery, a square of grass and cypress trees over which the tower-block banking buildings of Wilshire Boulevard cast a day-long shadow, Den did his tour-guide bit. He pointed out the graves of Marilyn's sometime boss, Darryl Zanuck, who I was pleased to see came from the fine-sounding town of Wahoo, Nebraska, and Roy Orbison, Truman Capote, Natalie Wood and the girl from *Poltergeist*, whose name escapes me.

When we came to Marilyn's corner Den raised his eyebrows and tilted his head towards the singing Marilyn lookalike in a kind of 'get in there my son' way and wandered off.

This was easier gestured about than done. So I sat for a while behind her on the concrete bench set here by a Marilyn fan club and listened to her crooning to herself.

Others came and went. Most came across to this corner, identified the marble-fronted pigeon-hole, one row in and one row up, which houses Marilyn, took a picture or posed for one, and went. It is just one of thirty or so identical compartments in only one section of the catacombs that run along one boundary of the cemetery: a strikingly egalitarian resting place.

Den got very indignant on Marilyn's behalf about this simple crypt in this tiny cemetery blocked in on all sides by high-rises. 'She's only the most famous woman in the world,' he said. 'You'd think they could make some effort.'

The woman at the crypt showed no sign of moving. She just sat, her purse and car keys on the concrete before her feet, crooning and rocking gently. The sprinklers had been on that morning, and even before

33

the sun found the lawn, the mid-summer temperatures caused the grass to steam a little.

Suddenly I was startled by a woman's anguished cry coming from the far side of the cemetery. I turned, expecting another disturbed lookalike, but instead saw a funeral procession. A crocodile of people in black followed an ornate white coffin with gold fittings. They moved towards a mound of earth covered in a green tarpaulin. The widow, crying and beseeching, was held by a young man at each forearm. As the funeral party reached the graveside, undertakers brought elaborate floral tributes – red flowers shaped into giant hearts, yellow and white wreaths on easels – and ranged them behind the priest, who stood on the opposite side of the grave to the mourners.

As my eye scanned the cemetery I realized that there was a third person lingering here. A man in dark glasses, dressed in the sharply smart casual wear of Los Angeles, no socks under his deck shoes. He was leaning against a tree near the grave of Darryl Zanuck, and looking towards the woman and me.

I decided not to hang around, but before I left I wrote a note on the back of one of my cards and put it at the woman's feet. I said I was a writer and wanted to meet fans of Marilyn, and gave the number of my motel. She seemed not to notice me do it. Then I left. As I walked to the gate the man pushed himself away from his tree and cut across at an angle to intercept me halfway to the gates. He smiled, white teeth in a tanned face.

'No dice, huh?' he said to me.

'I'm sorry?'

'She didn't want to know?'

I guessed he thought I was trying to pick the Marilyn woman up, so I told him what I was doing.

'Well if you want to talk to fans you should talk to me,' he said, adding, 'now that I know you're not competition . . .' Then, looking over my shoulder, he said, 'Well hi.'

I turned to see Marilyn's mourner walking towards

us, my card in her hand. She was smiling. 'Listen,' she said to me, 'it would be great to talk, but right now I have to fly. I've got your number, I'll call you.'

'Shouldn't you tell him your name?' the man said to her on my behalf.

She half turned as she walked away and called over her shoulder, 'I'm Ruth.'

'Hey,' said the guy, 'that's a coincidence. I'm Ruthless!' And he winked at me with a little wiggle of his head to make sure I appreciated his wit.

She gave him a smile of sympathy, then hurried off over the moist grass that seemed man-made, woven in a soft green web over the hard earth. He watched her all the way to the gate. Then he told me what he was doing here. He was trying to pick up Marilyn lookalikes. One of the best places to meet her doubles was at the crypt, he said, which struck me as a pretty bizarre pick-up point. But no, he said, he had met dozens of women here. Sometimes it led just to one dinner and no further, but often things clicked.

Double paydirt. Two crazies in one visit! Things could not be better.

As this guy, who told me his name was Victor, eased into his chat, he revealed the arrogance of the terminally stupid.

'I understand women like Marilyn,' he said in the coffee shop he steered me to round the corner. Basically she was insecure, he said, unsure of herself, craving love. She'd come from a broken home, never knew her father. 'You know she had a picture of Clark Gable on her bedroom wall when she was a kid, and used to fantasize that he was her father. Well, there's a bit of the Clark Gable in me,' and he grinned, sipping from his iced water. I assumed he meant the sticky-out ears. 'They like a guy who can wrap 'em up and sweep 'em away.'

He would use contact magazines too, he said, advertising for Marilyn lookalikes. 'I'll put something like "You're my Marilyn I'm your Joe" or "JFK seeks MM".

Women like Marilyn are old-fashioned,' he went on, 'they like to be taken care of, they want the gifts, to go out on the town. And in return they give you their bodies. That's what Marilyn did, she'd put out for a guy as a kind of thank-you.'

In Victor's case it would be probably as a kind of 'thank you for not giving me any more of your particularly noxious brand of bullshit.'

'Every man's dream is to make love with Marilyn Monroe,' he went on. 'I can't do that, but sometimes I get pretty close.'

What, I thought, closer than an inflatable?

'And,' he went on, waggling his head again, 'when a chick who looks just like Marilyn calls you Mr President in a cracked little voice at that special time. . . ' He paused, raising his eyebrows and sinking his chin in an expression of extreme significance.

'You know your name is Bill Clinton?' I asked.

He gave a dry, humourless chuckle.

'What Marilyn chicks really get a kick out of,' he went on, 'is something with a link to what she did. If you take them somewhere, maybe even if you say I'll meet you on Marilyn's star in Hollywood Boulevard, they'll get a kick out of that. Her star is right outside McDonald's, so what you can do right away if it's early – I've done this a number of times – is you say I'm taking you for champagne breakfast by Marilyn's star and you go in, get a couple of egg Macmuffins or what have you, and the chick is thinking, I don't call this a champagne breakfast, but then she finds you've snuck a bottle in and a couple of Styrofoam cups and you have got her the champagne breakfast. And it's like you're two young lovers with not a lot of dough but having a whole heap of fun. You should try it, kid,' he said as he slid the check across the table to me, and stood to leave.

It was early on the morning of 4 August, the last day Marilyn saw, when Ruth called me to fix a time to meet. She would come to me, she said, so we settled on breakfast at a lunch counter near my motel. I was staying on the ocean in Santa Monica, which I hoped would be cooler than somewhere inland. In the early mornings it could be quite chilly, before the sun burned the sea fog away.

The motel was decidedly low-rent, but it offered cheap weekly rates, and would make a good base on the numerous occasions over the coming months on which I would need to be in L.A. It could have been worse. There could have been a dead body in the bed. Worse still, there could have been Victor in the bed.

I was usually woken early. Yesterday it had been an insistent dull thudding which proved to be a kid bouncing a basketball against the other side of the ash-block wall by my head. Smack smack smack. On other mornings a couple of Mexicans would decide at dawn to empty the bottles from a neighbouring restaurant into a large metal skip. Sometimes, in the middle of the night, they would break up cardboard boxes by energetically kicking them around the small concrete yard behind my room. It was a curious little corner. In all the sad mess of boxes and bottles and rubbish, a lemon tree flourished, its boughs heavy with healthy green fruit just showing the first tinges of yellow. One afternoon I bought gin and tonic water from the local liquor store, cut a lemon from the tree, packed a tall glass with ice, made my drink and sat out by the pool, watching the waterboatmen stroke themselves along in the dirty water.

The sun had not yet penetrated the fog, and I shivered as I waited for Ruth at the lunch counter just east of my hotel along Ocean Avenue. I liked the faded seaside air of Santa Monica, with its pier complete with rifle range and side stalls, hot-dog stands and throngs of fishermen; its row of sorry-looking Fifties motels with their brave neon signs and grand names: the Ocean Sands, the Desert Sands and the Bayside Inn.

The lunch counter was on one edge of a triangle

of dead grass on which six palm trees put up with a sculpture that looked like two giant slices of concrete melon. On another side of the triangle was a clapped-out row of grey wooden apartments. On the balcony of the first floor was a notice: Hungarian Music Lesson and, against the end wall, a huge blue neon sign: Thrifty. This was just the way I felt, living here.

Ruth came late, wearing the black slacks I had seen her in at the crypt, and over her T-shirt a thick wrap-over cardigan with a belt similar to one I had seen Marilyn wearing in some of the photos from the final session of her life, with George Barris, in June and July 1962.

Objectively, Ruth looked nothing like Marilyn, though she had done everything she could with hair colouring and cosmetics to create a similarity. Her chin was too weak, her forehead too broad and her lips too thin. And she had a singsong voice and a saccharine giggle which I expected to find singularly irritating but to my surprise were actually rather endearing.

She had a glass of milk and said, 'OK. We're gonna make this a Marilyn day. This whole day is going to be like a memorial to Marilyn. We're gonna go to all the special Marilyn places – which I will show you – and we're gonna just think all the time about Marilyn and what a great lady she was and what a fine actress and stuff.'

Oh, I said. That sounds nice. I said I'd like to go to the grave again, but she said no, not today.

'Today it will be horrible at Westwood. And I mean horrible. It will be crawling with people. The Press always ruin Marilyn's anniversary, and her birthday too, pushing and shoving and sticking their cameras in your face and their microphones up your nose and stuff.'

I pointed out that it was tomorrow when the big event, the memorial service, was planned for the cemetery. It was actually on 5 August that Marilyn died, albeit very early in the morning, and that was the day when she would be on the TV news and so on. But Ruth was adamant.

'Believe me,' she said. 'I know a lot of real special places which will tell you a whole lot more about Marilyn.'

I told her I'd already done the Marilyn tour with Den but she said oh no, this would be different.

She was right. While Den had kept a discreet distance, observing the local ordinances, fearful of the 'massive ticket' he would get if he nosed his Caddy up to the doors of Marilyn's former homes, Ruth was right on in there.

We picked up the car and drove east.

Ruth told me about herself. She was a receptionist in a dental surgery in Van Nuys. She was thirty-one, had been married for five years to a fireman called Jim but that had ended two years ago, and now she lived alone with a cat called Joe DiMaggio.

'Joe DiMaggio?'

'Yes. I did have a real cute little cat called Arthur Miller but he got splatted in the street.'

As we cruised along Hollywood Boulevard I remembered to turn and see if the fog had burned off enough to reveal the Hollywood sign high to the north. I looked at it every time I passed, like touching a lucky charm in my pocket. Den had told me how you were supposed to see Hollywood for the first time. At Hollywood and Vine, he said, you should be blindfolded, then marched along to Grauman's (now Mann's) Chinese Theatre, where the stars have imprinted their hands and feet in wet cement and where Marilyn is supposed to have suggested she leave the imprint of her backside. There the blindfold is removed. Welcome to Hollywood! The manager of Levi and the Rockettes had introduced his boys to the city just like that, said Den.

Ruth directed me to El Centro, a run-down neighbourhood just to the east of the bright-lights big-city stretch of Hollywood Boulevard, with its rows of souvenir shops. She told me to pull up outside the ochre walls of the Orphans' Home Society building.

I knew that Marilyn, or Norma Jeane as she then was, had never known her father and that her mother, Gladys Baker, had suffered from the family curse of mental illness. She had been largely unable to look after Marilyn as a child. For some of the time she found foster homes for her daughter, but for twenty-one formative months Marilyn stayed here. It was a period during which the sense of being unwanted and unloved was forever imprinted upon her, and helped stoke the craving for love and attention which drove her as an adult. For the first three years of her career, while her mother resided in an asylum, Marilyn denied her existence, claiming to be an orphan.

Ruth marched straight in.

'Hi,' she said, in that singsong voice. 'We are big fans of Marilyn Monroe and we'd like to see her room please.'

The middle-aged black man in Reception began to rise from behind his desk. 'I'm sorry,' he said, 'but we cannot allow you to just walk in. This is an orphanage.'

'Oh please please please,' said Ruth, dropping her shoulders and holding her hands out, palms up, towards him. 'I know the kids are all at school. We just want a peek. This guy has come all the way from England . . .'

The man looked from her to me.

'I've no idea which room it is . . .' he began, in a tone that told Ruth she had won.

'I do, I do,' she said, and gave a little skip of excitement. 'It's on the second floor, right up in the right-hand corner of the building.'

He led the way, up institutional stairs, along a corridor that smelt of children and disinfectant, and opened the door of a room that contained four beds, four lockers and very little else.

Ruth went straight to the window.

'See that?' she asked me, pointing to a concrete tower which I seemed to recall from the titles of childhood television series.

'That's the globe on the top of RKO studios. Marilyn would look right across to it and daydream about one day going over there. Then when she was six all the orphans were invited to a Christmas party and Marilyn got a string of fake pearls, which she kept with her always, right until she died. Just think. Marilyn looked at that view every day.'

We left, drove on down the street and stopped outside the Holly Grove Thrift Store. 'Marilyn wore clothes bought from here,' said Ruth, and took me inside. She riffled through the racks, then came upon a cardboard box of plastic jewellery and picked out three big black bracelets which she bought, for $2, and slipped on her wrist. She called it getting in the Marilyn mood.

Ruth knew everything about her idol. As we drove she talked a non-stop Marilyn biog. At sixteen, perhaps because she craved a sense of belonging to somebody, was desperate to shrug off her orphan status, Marilyn married the twenty-one-year-old son of a neighbour, Jim Dougherty. The marriage lasted four years, during which time Jim joined the Merchant Marine and was away for long stretches.

At the age of twenty, having become a successful model and been signed by 20th Century-Fox, Norma Jeane reinvented herself as Marilyn Monroe. She shut the door on her childhood, her marriage, on all her past life, and was reborn. 'Like a beautiful butterfly emerging from a chrysalis,' said Ruth.

'Are you in the Marilyn mood yet?' she asked me, with great seriousness.

I told her I was pretty sure I was on the way to being in a Marilyn mood but that we should maybe work on it a little more.

So we did. We stopped on Sunset Boulevard for the Parisienne Florists where, Ruth told me, Joe DiMaggio had placed an order for fresh flowers to be put on Marilyn's grave three times a week for six years. We went for lunch at Barney's Beanery, an unprepossessing wooden shack on Santa Monica Boulevard with three pool tables and 200 different beers. It was here, Ruth told me, that Marilyn came after the famous nude calendar sessions she did aged twenty-three in 1949.

'She got $50,' said Ruth, 'and she was so broke and it was such a big pile of dough that she came here and had chilli and fries to celebrate.' The calendar, with her on a red velvet drape, was on sale still in the souvenir stores on Hollywood Boulevard.

We took a stroll around those stores in the afternoon. They were full of Marilyn Monroe merchandise. There were posters, mugs, sweatshirts; everything with her image on it. She stood alongside James Dean and Elvis, who also had their faces on a hundred different items, as if they were a trinity. Ruth took me to another store, then another. Marilyn's face was everywhere.

In this third shop there was a curious poster. It was a pastiche of the cover of the Beatles' *Abbey Road*. In the photograph on the album the four Beatles walk across a zebra crossing in Abbey Road, London. In this version the places were taken by Elvis, Marilyn, James Dean and, rather uncertainly bringing up the rear, Humphrey Bogart.

I objected to this feeble number four.

'Who would you put there?' Ruth asked me. 'Kennedy,' I said. 'Then you have the Supergroup.'

'Hmmm,' she said, thinking about it. 'I'm not sure whether Kennedy was a good guy or a bad guy.'

I asked Ruth how often she went out to the crypt. 'Maybe once a week,' she answered. 'I guess I sort of meditate. I can't really tell you conscious thoughts. But I think about Marilyn, about how if I had been around then and was her friend I could have saved her. Because she was so alone, all her life. But I don't just think of her as a victim, a dumb blonde who couldn't cope. She was an amazing lady. She had her own production

42

company when it was unheard-of for an actor to have such a thing – let alone a woman. And think of the men she knew. She married Joe DiMaggio who was a real sporting hero, Arthur Miller who is a great playwright, she had relationships with John Kennedy, Robert Kennedy, Frank Sinatra, Yves Montand – who was just about the biggest singer in Europe at the time . . .'

And she talked as if of a close friend, about Marilyn's struggles to make it, and being dropped by two major studios, having affairs with two much older men – Freddy Karger, a musician, and Johnny Hyde, a hugely influential Hollywood agent who was the architect of her early success.

Then it was on to Beverly Hills and the little wooden shingled house that she and Joe DiMaggio returned to after their wedding in 1954 when she was twenty-seven. 'There is a wonderful picture,' said Ruth, 'of Marilyn standing right here on the sidewalk, wearing a bathrobe, with a bottle of milk and a newspaper in her hand.' She hopped out and stood in the spot. 'There's an old lady there now aged about ninety-eight. I don't think she knows who Marilyn Monroe is.'

As she spoke the door to the house swung open and an elderly woman stood watching us.

'Clear off or I'll call the cops,' she shouted.

'Shut the door you goddam fucking bitch!' screamed Ruth with a vehemence which startled me, and the old lady. The door closed, and Ruth got back into the car.

'It's OK,' she said. 'We always have words. It don't mean nothing.'

'So you come here a lot too?'

'Now and then. It's Marilyn's happiest place. When she lived here she was the coming thing, she'd made *Gentlemen Prefer Blondes*, which was just brilliant, and she'd married the most eligible man in America.'

Ruth wanted to round off the day by doing something really special, a Marilyn-mood thing that she had never done before. She told me she had had a brainwave. Joe and Marilyn had spent their first night as husband

43

and wife in a motel on the outskirts of Paso Robles, up the coast from L.A. on Highway 101. Just south of there was a kitsch castle of a hotel called the Madonna Inn. It was the kind of place where Liberace would feel at home, a Disneyland for grown-ups where the rooms were themed as anything from a caveman's lair to a mountain cabin. The dining-room had gilt cherubs, heart-shaped tables and a dance floor where middle-aged couples would shuffle around to a jazz band so laid back they were almost catatonic. We would go there for dinner.

The drive up the coast, often right alongside the ocean, was pleasantly cool in the baking afternoon, with the sea scent filling the hot air. But as the afternoon turned into evening Ruth's conversation tailed off.

'This is the hardest part of any day of the year for me,' she said. 'Marilyn would have taken the barbiturates that killed her about now,' she went on, 'or had them administered.'

I could see this evening was going to be a whole bundle of laughs.

In the dining-room of the Madonna Inn, red like a womb, the old-timers filled the red plastic bench seats which curved around the tables. At the one next to ours the couple had a purple balloon nudging the ceiling. It had Happy Birthday written on it. Middle-aged waitresses in milkmaid frocks and horn-rimmed spectacles took the orders, and brought bowls of appetizers that were like meals in themselves – a pile of salad, raw vegetables, salami and cheese.

I tried to keep the conversation light, but Ruth was sinking into a real Marilyn depression.

'She'd be getting wobbly now,' said Ruth, ordering a martini and – drinking it quickly – ordering another. 'I've read all the books and whatever the theories of the author, whether it was suicide, murder or an accidental overdose, they all have the timings about the same.'

All of a sudden tears welled from her eyes and

splashed on her plate. The waitress was perturbed. 'Can I get you anything, honey?' she asked.

Suddenly a retort like a gunshot had us all involuntarily ducking our heads. Ruth let out a yell and the waitress turned to the scene of the commotion. 'Balloon,' she said, 'balloon.' The next-door couple's birthday balloon had gone pop. They were given a yellow one to replace it. At least Ruth was smiling again.

Our food arrived and we began to eat. A four-piece band had moved onto the stage on the far side of the dance floor, and was playing away quietly: background mood music that was barely noticeable. Ruth was getting more and more morose: 'Marilyn would be stumbling around her room now. They found a bruise on her back, a fresh one where she had crashed into a nightstand or something. And there was a stack of records on the record player. Frank Sinatra playing her out.'

A female singer had joined the band, and they were doing 'Crazy', an old Patsy Cline number. How appropriate, I thought. If I'd known I would have asked them to dedicate the number to Ruth, who was now sitting in silence, her plate untouched before her.

The band played 'My Heart Belongs to Daddy', which Marilyn sang in *Let's Make Love*, and Ruth said we had to dance. I told her I couldn't but she said it didn't matter. And it didn't, because she was pretty drunk by now and the best she could do was shuffle slowly round and round. Halfway through the song Ruth asked to sit down again. She said she was sorry but she just kept thinking of Marilyn lying in her room, naked, the phone off the hook, slowly dying. And there was no-one to help her. How she wished she could reach her. She cried again.

'I have this crazy feeling that if I was alive then we would have been friends and I could have done something,' she said.

About midnight we began the two-hour drive back to

L.A. As we got to the outskirts of the city it was 2.15. At 3, Ruth mumbled to me, Eunice Murray, Marilyn's housekeeper, would awake and become alarmed that Marilyn's door was locked. She would call out, but could not rouse her. She would go into the garden, find the curtains open in Marilyn's bedroom and see her lying still on the bed. The story would be disputed, just as everything else about Marilyn's death has been over the years.

Ruth wanted to pass the house where Marilyn died, so we came off the freeway and went west on Sunset then south towards San Vicente Boulevard, passing the little dead-end streets which number twenty-five, each one of the Helena Drives. At Fifth Helena Drive we moved slowly down to the end house, 12305, hidden behind its high walls. This was the first house Marilyn ever owned. She bought it in 1961, the year before she died. It was tiny, with three small bedrooms, a minute lounge, dining-room and kitchen, and two bathrooms. But it had a pool behind the walls which ensured her privacy.

'How often do you come here?' I asked Ruth.

'Only once right up to the door,' she said. 'The guy who owns it is weird. He must be a fan because he paid twice the market price for it. It's a $1m house and he paid $2m, but he hates having fans around. He calls the cops if a tour bus comes up here. It's crazy, like living in Graceland and not allowing Elvis fans to come by. What time is it?'

I told her it was five past three. She yawned. 'OK,' she said, 'Marilyn is dead. I can go to sleep now.'

Next morning I was woken by the phone once more. And it was Ruth again, burbling about how it had been so so so SO good of me to put up with her last night and to get her through Marilyn's last day and how there were still a million things to show me so she would be right over . . .

Hold on, I thought. That's enough of that. In any

case, I had already decided to leave town on the first of my trips. I had a hankering just to drive. Feel my wheels eating up the miles. Cross the desert to Las Vegas for a little Elvis-crazy watching, then on up the lonely highway to Reno, to get into a different kind of Marilyn mood.

But I remembered Ruth, even over a year later, when I saw a one-paragraph Associated Press report about Marilyn's house in a London newspaper.

It read: 'Los Angeles: Michael Ritchie, a film director, has bought the house in which Marilyn Monroe was found dead in 1962. He plans to demolish the building and replace it with a bigger home.'

Over Ruth's dead body, I thought.

CHAPTER TWO

Marry me, Elvis

ELVIS PRESLEY,
LAS VEGAS, NEVADA

Up the aisle went Kyle and Laura. Up the aisle went Elvis. As the trio approached the altar, Elvis began to sing. He sang:

> 'Waaah muuuh suh
> ohhhlee fuuu ruh shin
> buuuh daah cahn hep
> fawlin in luuu wuuuh yuuuh'

And I sat at the back thinking wait a minute. There is something wrong here. Somebody should say something. It was that feeling you might get if you were the only sober one at a party and someone was about to do something really dangerous and you were the only one in a fit state to point it out. Or if you were in a car and it was going to crash, clearly going to crash, but the driver and the other passengers seem blithely unaware of the danger. And you think, he'll notice the truck, he'll see it any second, but he doesn't and pretty soon self-preservation is going to get the better of reticence and you will have to yell out AAAHHH! STOP! STOP! STOP!

I felt like I should say stop now. Say look, this is a wedding, this is no place for a fat man in Elvis drag. But I didn't say anything, because I knew that while I might think I was the only sane one in this asylum, by Las Vegas standards this was all totally sane and quite, quite normal.

Being in Las Vegas was like that. It was NOT real. Nothing here is real. In this unreal place even marriage is unreal. You can do it at midnight, on a whim. Takes ten minutes to get a licence. You can get spliced with a man pretending to be Elvis standing behind you, you could do it in a chapel just off a casino, leaving someone to feed your slot while you tied the knot.

No, Las Vegas was not real. It was better than real. It was ideal. Las Vegas represents an ideal life, for as long as the money lasts. You can have such a wonderful time, and get married in the middle of it and so make marriage part of the wonderful, unreal world of Las Vegas. You could probably marry your dog. Or a pizza, as long as the pizza was fourteen years old and the judge at the court-house thought it was mature enough for such a big step.

Las Vegas panders to man's real desires. Nevada in general, Las Vegas in particular, have got rich on permitting the things other states forbid. Gambling, prostitution, quick and easy marriage, fast divorce too if it doesn't work out.

Unfortunately you can't quite have Elvis marry you – Norm Jones is not qualified. But he specializes in the renewal of vows. Here's one he's real proud of: I Sally take you John to be my wedded husband, to always love you tender and never to return to sender.

And you can enter into the spirit of things. Norm had one couple go down the aisle of the Graceland Wedding Chapel dressed as convicts while he sang 'Jailhouse Rock' (Cuh-ma-dah-thah jah-hah rah wi mah), and instead of rings they exchanged ball and chain.

Ideally, I'd want Elvis as pastor, me as James Dean, the bride as Marilyn Monroe and JFK as the bride's father. Scarlett O'Hara would be outside, cursing that someone else got her man.

If you did want to point out the unreality of it all

in Vegas you could make a stand on the Strip at midnight, outside the Mirage where a volcano erupts every fifteen minutes – giant gusts of flame blasting out over the waterfalls and torrents so it looks as if the water is on fire. You could set up your soapbox by Treasure Island, where two full-size galleons sit at anchor in a medieval harbour. You could hand out leaflets by the Showboat, a building modelled like a giant paddle steamer covered in lights which hoots every few minutes. You could yell 'This is not real, wake up!' and you'd be the crazy one.

You could go up to the crowd outside the Candle-light Chapel, which marries twenty-four hours a day, jamming them in so tight that the pavement outside is a permanent crush of rival brides and grooms, best men and matrons of honour, and tell them it is all horrible, tasteless, awful, and you'd be the weird one. Because this is wonderland, never-never land, Erewhon, Nowhere, paradise, heaven.

I was grateful to Las Vegas, because it put me on the right track, helped me get things in perspective. I'd been puzzling over the Marilyn people I had met – Victor and Ruth – and thinking they were odd, to say the least. But in Vegas I began to see things differently. Maybe they were not the sad inadequates they had seemed in L.A. Perhaps I should not think of them as rather pitiable people whose personalities were so underdeveloped that they had to live their lives through a dead star.

The best way to get into my subject, I decided, was to see Victor and Ruth as normal, and myself as the weird one. The only reason I found them strange at first, I told myself, was because I had been living my life on a lower plane. These obsessives were on a higher plane, and much more in tune with reality. Having a lot more fun. Or at least, that's what it felt like in Vegas's world, where the rules are the city's own creation.

Las Vegas had been beckoning me from the heart of L.A. ever since I had arrived there. From the Santa

Monica Boulevard close to my motel the first of the freeway billboards trumpeted: 'Excalibur, all rooms $49' under a picture of a hotel that looked like a fairytale castle. There were billboards for Luxor, too, a giant black-glass pyramid with a huge sphinx in front. The slogan was 'You won't believe your eyes'. And it was true. Lord, it was all true.

As I chased out through L.A. and across the desert towards Nevada the billboards beckoned me on. The signs got bigger and the prices got lower. 'Rooms $18!!!' 'Rooms $10 including two meals.' 'Free food.' 'Unlimited shrimp.' 'Sex with Marilyn.'

OK, I made that last one up.

On the state line a bunch of kids with advanced construction skills had built two mirage-like casinos and hotel complexes. One was a pretend Wild West town, the other a foretaste of the Showboat, both plonked down in the middle of the desert. When Vegas itself appears over the scrubby horizon it looks at first like a simple scattering of white blocks. But then, low but growing until finally they loom over you like an hallucination, come the giant black pyramid of Luxor, Excalibur's multi-coloured ice-cream-cone-and-onion turrets, and the sheer cream bulk of Caesar's Palace.

By day, you see right through the whole place. Like a movie-set street of flat store fronts, the Strip has nothing much beyond it. You can look down the side streets, past a few nondescript buildings, to an expanse of desert and the mountains in the distance. By day, man's playful extravagance is dwarfed, belittled by nature. The thing to do is arrive gritty from the six-hour drive across the desert at dusk, shower, then go out at nightfall. Stay up all night, sleep the daylight hours away.

And when I got here I found all the promises on the billboards came true. Someone was giving me free money. At Bob Stupak's Vegas World you get a free $50 Casino Bankroll, $20 for the tables, $30 for dollar slot-machines. The slots got my adrenalin flowing. After a few pumps around a number of machines I found one I liked. It felt lucky. After a couple of goes I got a little win, and felt sure there was a big jackpot there, I just had to coax it out. But then you get all the losers with their plastic cups full of change sniffing out a lucky streak. They come hovering, hoping you'll get bored and move on.

I got a second little pay-out and kept pushing in the quarters. I knew the big one was just around the corner but my plastic cup was almost empty and the roving change-maker nowhere in sight. I knew I couldn't leave the slot or one of the vultures would have it. I folded a bill longways and held it above my head, looking around, but the change trolley was nowhere to be seen. Two old ladies closed in on me, muttering, 'C'mon, you had your go, quit hogging the machine. You out of change it's time to give somebody else a turn.'

I had one coin left. It was mashed and the machine had spat it out when I had tried it before, but this time I balanced it in the slot and thumped it home. It worked. I punched the knob. Nothing. I was beaten.

There were plenty of other things free in Las Vegas apart from money. I could get free poker lessons at any number of places, and a free Margarita at the Hacienda. At Lady Luck I could have the world's biggest hot dog. It was a foot long, weighed half a pound, was all beef and cost nothing. I could even get four free beers at the Holy Cow brewery. If food wasn't free it was very cheap. At the Riviera in the early hours I could have all the flapjacks I could eat, and all the coffee I could drink, for $1.99.

After bread there were circuses. At Circus Circus the show went on almost alongside the slot-machines – trapeze artists, high-wire acts, stunt cyclists. At Excalibur's multi-tiered dinner-theatre, King Arthur's Arena, I could watch jousting tournaments while I ate. At the Mirage, five dolphins swam in a $14m pool filled with what was described as 1.5 million gallons of man-made sea water. Man-made? At the Imperial

Palace I could admire Hitler's 1939 Mercedes, or the King of Siam's '28 Delage. If I got bored and needed a break I could fly to the Grand Canyon and eat a barbecue lunch prepared by Hualapai Indians.

At Harrah's there was a show called Spellbound, a Concert of Illusion, advertised with posters of a woman in fishnets and a minimalist leotard resting one elbow on a chrome pole with her legs crossed and elevated way above her head, while a man in leather trousers and a Bacofoil cardi ran a blazing hoop up and down her legs. Incredible! How DOES she keep that half-inch strip of material centred over her crotch?

You want culture, you want museums? OK, try the Liberace Museum. See the hotpants outfit he wore for the tribute to the 100th birthday of the Statue of Liberty. Have your picture taken with the VW kit car with Rolls-Royce radiator grille which was driven on stage at Radio City Music Hall to collect the maestro's cape. Admire the oil painting of Liberace in sober grey suit kneeling before the Pope and kissing his ring. Ignore the comments from the four gay men who precede you about that being by no means the only 'ring' Liberace kissed in a long and flamboyant life.

'Look at that picture,' said the guide, of another oil painting of the twinkly-eyed one, 'those eyes follow you around the room.' They did, I checked. They never left my backside for one minute.

Then there were Liberace's crown jewels, including the candelabra ring with platinum candlesticks and diamond flames, and a piano-shaped ring containing 260 diamonds and ivory and jade keys.

'He sure had a lot of purdy things, didn't he?' said one visitor to another.

If you were going to marry in Las Vegas you should definitely buy the wedding ring in Liberace's gift shop. You could even get married at his former home, Las Vegas Villa.

Marriage Las Vegas style fascinated me. I counted forty-three wedding chapels in the phone book and learned that 1,500 ceremonies take place a week, 80,000 a year. The chapels boasted of the stars they had spliced. A Little White Chapel had a sign boasting 'Joan Collins ♥ Michael Jordan', and offered the one and only drive-up wedding window in the world. Bride to go, everything on it, large Coke, small fries.

The Temple of Human Kindness offered 'Mike the marrying man' alias Ottawa Indian chief Michael Ben Michael. 'Not religious but very caring to your needs . . . with the most beautiful sacred ancient Ottawa Indian marriage agreement in the world.'

I went into the Hitching Post Chapel to find out about weddings. There was a wishing well out front, and a sign saying they spoke English, French, Polish, Russian and Spanish. I explained that I wanted to talk about marriage in the town, but it seemed the person who spoke English was not in today.

'Ah, Elvis, Viva Las Vegas here,' said the non-English speaker.

'Elvis was married here?' I asked, knowing that he was not. She nodded: 'Uh huh. You have girl?'

'Er, no, that's not what . . .'

'She eighteen years old?'

'Er, no, look . . .'

'She sixteen parents' consent. She fifteen, fourteen, court order. Can do. And please $50. You are ready now for marriage?'

'Do you have wedding clothes?'

'Yes, yes.'

'Jump suits?'

'Jump suits no have.'

'Forget it then.'

I went down the Strip to the Wee Kirk of the Heather.

'That's Irish,' said the Imelda Marcos lookalike in Reception. 'It means Little Church in the Flowers. I'm Lynette. That's French.'

Just then we were interrupted. In came a man in T-shirt and jeans and a woman with long blond hair, a short white button-through dress and white hold-up stockings laddered above the knee.

I sat out by a fridge full of flower arrangements while they stood before Lynette's desk, the man pawing the woman's arse as they answered Lynette's questions.

'You want a wedding garter, Jan?' asked Lynette.

'Oh lemme see do we want one Jimmy?'

Jimmy could barely contain himself.

'The peach one is kinda purdy,' he suggested.

Jan sat down and slid it up her right leg, adjusting it well above the knee but not far enough up to be obscured by the short white dress.

Jimmy gave her a look that suggested it was a toss-up whether they'd be getting into the consummation before or after the service.

'You can keep it on tonight,' he growled. 'Won't that be a trip?'

Lynette tried to keep the conversation light. 'Have you seen the Mirage and the volcano erupt at night yet? You don't want to miss that.'

I was wondering whether we'd be seeing Jimmy erupt any second.

'We have to get back,' said Jan. 'We came all the way out here from San Diego this morning and our limo driver is very expensive.'

I noticed through the lace curtains that they had a stretch purring in the parking lot.

'I have to go to work at six. I'm a dancer, and we won't see each other at all. I'll be gone all night and he'll be gone all day.'

Lynette asked them if they'd like to go out for a puff while they awaited the pastor, and Jimmy dragged Jan back into the limo.

But it was when I saw the Graceland Chapel that I knew I had hit the essence of marriage, Las Vegas style.

While he waited for Kyle and Laura, I talked to Norm Jones in a little side room filled with ribbons and a TV tuned to the baseball. 'Yep,' he said, 'marriage is big business, second only to the hotel and casino trade. You got over 80,000 weddings a year, and every licence costs $35 and has to be got from the courthouse. I charge $100, and it's $50 for the video, say $250 on average per wedding.'

And Norm, who also doubles as clerk and janitor at the chapel, has done as many as fourteen Elvis weddings in a day. That's $1,400! This afternoon he was going to run through eight. It was enough to make anyone think twice about laughing at a fat man with his hair dyed black wearing a white jump suit slashed to the navel.

I half hoped Kyle and Laura would turn as he followed them down the aisle and say, 'No, there's been a mistake. We ordered the young Elvis, not the one bloated on prescription drugs and junk food. Take this wreck away.'

But they didn't, of course, and after Norm's opening number pastor Rudi Aquila, a sort of Latin Sammy Davis Junior, was into his spiel: 'I recall the story of a young couple, got married. They were on their honeymoon, walking on the beach in the evening. The husband kind of looked in her eyes and said, "You realize in fifty years we'll be celebrating our golden wedding anniversary." That husband certainly had the right idea.'

The rings were exchanged, and the kisses, and it was back to Norm, who switched on a taped backing track and said where you folks from, which was Chicago, and then said, 'Well let's put a little bit of Las Vegas into Chicago,' and sang 'Viva Las Vegas', or 'Vuh-vuh La Veyha'. Then he introduced 'All Shook Up' ('which I guess is what you're feelin' right now Kyle') and got the groom to join in.

At one point Norm nipped back up the aisle and returned with a red satin scarf around his neck. It had Graceland Wedding Chapel printed on it in black and he draped it around Laura's neck. Then he sang 'Memories' and got the couple up dancing, while the congregation stood up, snapped his picture and whooped. Then there were the wedding photos, just the principals, just Kyle and Laura and Elvis.

And I got that feeling of being the only sane one in an asylum again. Imagine being shown these wedding photos. You'd have to say, 'Hey, Kyle, mate, there's something wrong with these. I mean, this is you, right, and this is Laura, but what's with the fat guy in white? No, don't tell me. Elvis came back from the dead, right, and he married Laura, and you were the best man?'

The road to Reno was perfection: 481 miles of lonesome highway threading through a desolate landscape, up through the Mojave and on to the Great Basin desert, through a landscape littered with decaying gold- and silver-mining towns, dried-up lakes and rivers that run to nowhere, just giving up and disappearing amid the dry scrub. This is the last, vast, rugged and remote wild country in the USA, where you can trek for hundreds of miles on gravel roads and not see another soul, or as much as a house, for days.

For the first 200 miles up I-95 – the Bonanza Highway – I was zipping through the low-lying Mojave, where creosote bushes offer about the only vegetation. To my right, stretching virtually the whole way to the crossroads town of Fallon, was the vast restricted zone of the Nellis Air Force Range where the Stealth bomber was test-flown and where, in the cold war, Soviet MiG jet fighters brought by defecting pilots gave up their secrets.

The little towns were there to serve the road – places like Indian Springs with their motel, gas stations and perhaps a low-rent casino. At Mercury, entrance to the Nevada Test Site, where underground nuclear testing takes place, a cluster of protesters sat in the shade of a great hulking beast known as a recreational vehicle. The highway authorities prepare you for their presence with a sign reading 'Demonstrators on roadway 25mph'.

At Goldfield I pulled in to take a look at a virtual ghost town. Gold was discovered here at the turn of the century, in a strike so rich that miners who were paid a daily wage of $5 could hide – or 'high grade' – $250 worth of nuggets a day in their shoes, secret pockets and hollowed-out axe handles and sell it to fences for cash. This was truly serious money, and within months a railroad had been forced through the desert and a range of substantial stone buildings were thrown up – a bank, court-house, school and hotel – to give the place an instant solidity.

By 1910, at the height of the boom, production topped $11 million a year, but the seam began to give out soon afterwards. There was a major flood in Goldfield in 1913 and a fire in 1923 which left it almost a ghost town. This is what it still is today, its population down from 20,000 to 400. Little evidence is left of the heyday, little except the boarded-up and abandoned three-storey Goldfield High School, and the Goldfield Hotel, built for half a million dollars in 1908 but bankrupt and closed since 1946.

A sign that was too old to be reliable took me past the school to the Santa Fe Saloon. I half expected it to have been abandoned too, but it turned out to be one of the few still-functioning relics of the gold rush with its wooden board floors, a cool back bar and a Jolly Joker antique poker-pinball machine. On the wall was a pieced-together photograph of Goldfield in its prime, when it still covered fifty blocks, rather than the four or so it spans today. Out back were the cribs where the prostitutes once took a little gold from the miners.

At Tonopah the landscape changed as I moved from the Mojave to the Great Basin. But not a lot. All that happened was I swapped creosote for sage-brush, which at least gave a tang to the furnace-hot air that whipped past my wide-open windows. I won't use the air-conditioning in the desert. Call me old-fashioned, but what's the point of driving all day in such aridity unless you have to suffer some discomfort from it? It was certainly exhausting, with the temperature in the high nineties.

The country got greener as I moved further north. And there was water – at least at Walker Lake, eight miles wide and thirty miles long, which I came to after descending through the valley around Hawthorne, which is a vast ammunition dump. The landscape around Hawthorne is taken up totally by the US Army Ammunition Plant, and thickly dotted with thousands of thick concrete bunkers about the size of Nissen huts. They are filled with every conceivable kind of ammunition – bullets, bombs, grenades, mortars, mines, and missiles. This is the USA's arsenal.

I stopped at Walker Lake, which though it seems like a vast expanse of water in such an arid setting, is actually the piddling remnant of ancient Lake Lahontan, which once covered 8,400 square miles of western Nevada and eastern California. Lying down in some shade by the lake I foolishly fell asleep, awaking to discover the sun had moved, pulling my shade away, and leaving me lobster pink and with my lips cracking.

Back in the car I soon started shivering, felt sick and realized that, like a mad dog of an Englishman, I had managed to get sunstroke. But there was nothing for it but to put my foot down, press on to Reno and find a motel as soon as possible. It was well after dark when I arrived and I seemed to have hit town at a busy time. The motels along the main drag of Virginia Street all had their No Vacancy signs lit. I cruised up, down and back again with no luck, and was beginning to despair of finding anything when I spotted a place with a vacancy.

I only vaguely noticed its name – Fantasy Inn. True, it was a little odd that the lobby seemed to double as a women's underwear store, and I was surprised to be given a complimentary bottle of champagne-style wine with my room key. But it wasn't until I let myself into my room that I realized exactly what kind of a place this was. There were mirrors at the foot and head of the bed, on the ceiling and all around the whirlpool bath which sat in the corner like a whitewater-rafting-ride capsule from an adventure park. But no matter. I would wash off the desert dust and cool my burning skin in a cold bath. I ran the water and tried to puzzle out the various knobs and switches. I pressed one and suddenly the bath, which was half-full, began to pump two strong jets of water right over the rim, soaking the wall, the carpet and my suitcase, which happened to be in the way.

I struggled with the knobs but could not get the water to stop pumping out across the room. Eventually I managed it, but not before almost the entire contents of the bath had been transferred onto the floor. I re-ran the bath and got in, finally easing the pain of too much driving and too much sun. But it was hard to relax, watching my shellfish-pink reflection in all four walls and the ceiling. So I turned the light off, sank back in the darkened tub and sang to myself, as Elvis might:

> 'Waaah muuuh suh
> ohhhlee fuuu ruuu shin
> buuuh daah cahn hep
> fawlin in luuu wuuuh yuuuh'

Eventually the lovebirds in the next room banged on the wall. Funny, I thought, not only could Elvis marry you, he could put you off your stroke as well.

CHAPTER THREE

Half Man, Half Marilyn

MARILYN MONROE,
RENO, NEVADA

I was trying to work out, as Michelle Grimes came trip-
ping from her car across my motel parking lot, whether
it was only because I had been expecting a transvestite
to turn up that she looked like a man in drag. I didn't
know for sure that she was not a woman. All I had to
go on, apart from the evidence of my own eyes, was the
fact that Roman Hyrniszak, who ran a Marilyn fan club
in Los Angeles and had put me in touch with Michelle,
had told me about his suspicions.

Roman had said that even at first, when he had
just heard her breathy little voice on the phone, he
had wondered. Then she had sent him a picture of
herself and he had thought hum, and shown it to his
girlfriend. 'Is this a guy?' he had asked, and they had
decided that, on balance, it probably was.

So when Michelle came mincing from her car to meet
me I was on the lookout for those giveaway masculine
traits. Her walk had a spot of the Dick Emerys about
it. The walk came from the posture: head held back
and sunk down on the neck; shoulders back and spine
locked; breasts thrust out, the body rocking from side
to side; hips moving as if powered by two short
pistons; tiny steps that made her white slingbacks
go click-click-click-click-click. And then the voice:
' Hi-I'm-Michelle-how-are-you-today?' delivered in the
soft, breathy tones of someone trying to take all the

masculine power out of their speech. If a man wanted to sound like a woman that's how he would go about it.

I looked closely at her. The make-up was thick. So were the neck, the waist and the ankles. But, hey, none of us is perfect, and there was no obvious giveaway, no visible stubble or Adam's apple. She wore a red blouse with bumps in the right place, a white skirt with red polka dots but without bumps in the wrong place, and tights. Tights, in this heat? Maybe she just liked to feel smart. There was an ankle bracelet under those tights and round that chunky ankle.

Suspicious, much of it, but not conclusive. I remembered that Marilyn, in the soft, breathless, vulnerable persona which she adopts in many of her film roles, has been described as more like a female impersonator than a real woman. Perhaps that was it. Whether male or female in the first place, Michelle was a Marilyn impersonator, from the short bleached and curled hair to the walk, the voice and the mannerisms.

But while I was checking her out, Michelle — as I discovered later — was checking me out. She was wondering whether it was quite safe to meet a man she knew nothing whatsoever about in his room at the Fantasy Inn. It was only after I had arranged the meeting that I discovered another of the room's delights was a TV showing two twenty-four-hour channels of hard porn, and realized that such a rendezvous point could be misconstrued by a girl. Or a man.

I decided that the thing to do was to be casually leaning against the car flicking through a guidebook when she arrived. Then I could say, hey, let's sit out by the pool and get to know each other. But the temperature was once again in the nineties, and she was nearly an hour late, and my sunstroke was making me feel decidedly queazy. So when she finally arrived I felt I was about to go into a dead faint. I did suggest, as I had planned to, that we sit out by the pool. But within seconds I could see her face was melting and she could see I was about to keel over. So, as we were planning that she should take me on a tour of the area, we got into my car and set the air-conditioning blasting.

After we had looked over the maps for a while I could see that she felt she had to ask what on earth I was doing in a sex motel on my own. I tried to tell her I was only here because I was a sick man, but I think she had reached that conclusion already. So we made a strange couple as we set out for downtown Reno – the transvestite sitting in fear of the pervert, the pervert in fear of the transvestite.

But I still couldn't be sure about that. Stepping out on the streets of Reno with Michelle, I watched for any evidence that would support my suspicion that she was a man. Would the gang of builders in hard hats walking past us give whoops of derision? They would not.

I had come to Reno simply because it was the setting for *The Misfits*, my favourite among Marilyn's films. It is the movie in which she plays a character closest to herself, and the last that she completed. *The Misfits* was written by Marilyn's then husband, Arthur Miller, and it comes over as a loving portrait by a man who could not hold her. Marilyn plays Roslyn, an only lightly-fictionalized version of herself, and the film is the story of a radiant, other-worldly woman with the power to inspire and transform all who come into contact with her.

It was a strangely doomed movie. Marilyn and Arthur Miller's four-year marriage – Marilyn's third – finally broke up during filming and, the day after it was completed, Clark Gable, Marilyn's co-star, suffered a massive heart attack, possibly brought on by the pressures of making the film. He died a few days later.

Marilyn's character has been staying in Reno for the six weeks necessary under lenient Nevada law to establish residency and qualify for divorce from her shiny-suited car-salesman husband. She falls in with three misfit cowboys who, loathing wages, prefer to get cash by taking part in rodeos and capturing wild horses – mustangs – once the workhorses of the West, without which the land could not have been settled. By 1960, however, when the film was made, mustangs were being sold for dogfood.

With curious symmetry, Gay, the cowboy she takes as her lover, is played by Clark Gable, who, as a little girl, Marilyn used to pretend was her father. The men are transfixed by Roslyn in the same way that the world remains transfixed by Marilyn. She seems to have the power to transform not just their lives but the world they live in. She is described as being newborn like a child. When they drive together, Gay says it feels an honour to be sitting next to her. When Gay's buddy Guido sees how she has fixed up the ranch he lends her, he says with awe that she has the gift for life.

Her sympathy is boundless. As Guido says, 'What happens to anybody happens to you.' She hates the thought of anything being killed, and the pain that she endures because of the suffering of others seems almost unbearable to her. She is very nearly too good – or too sensitive – for this world.

The opening scenes of the movie show Roslyn in the Reno boarding-house where she waits out her six weeks, which is where Michelle comes in. The scenes were filmed in a real boarding-house, run at the time of filming by Michelle's mother, in Liberty Street, just off Virginia Street.

We strolled past the site of the house, long since torn down to make way for a bank, and I remarked to Michelle: 'I guess at the time you were just a little . . .'

'. . . Kid,' she supplied for me, qualifying it with, 'Well, young teenager. It was such a thrill meeting Marilyn,' she went on. 'She was around just for a couple of days and I met her a couple of times after that. She was great, just great. I remember the day we met. It was 21 July 1960. I know she was going through a lot of emotional problems at the time, with her marriage collapsing, and I was in a bad way too. So we just had a mutual . . . something, I don't know what.

'I felt that she stabilized me, maybe saved my life. Just by being nice to me, giving me some affection. She took time to talk to me. We had a lot in common, she was an orphan and I was almost an orphan myself. My parents had split up when I was very young, I was away at boarding-school, I never saw my father, and Mom not for months at a time. Marilyn made a lasting impression on me, made me want to be her.'

She glanced at me, perhaps trying to gauge the impact of her words. I nodded in a way that I hoped was sympathetic, suggesting that, of course, who wouldn't. If I had met Marilyn as a child I'd probably be in a frock myself right now.

I was enjoying Reno, which was like Las Vegas's plain, unshowy little sister. Where Las Vegas is BIG on gambling, entertainment, spectacle, Reno goes for the quiet approach. There are casinos, clubs, topless bars and marriage parlours, but they are relatively discreet places. While Las Vegas is one big fun-filled neon migraine attack, Reno is sprinkled with cosy, dusty, 1950s glitter. If Reno was a person it would take a nap in the afternoon, occasionally forget to put its teeth in, and bore total strangers with pictures of its grandchildren.

At the top of Virginia Street, where the sign arching across the road reads The Biggest Little City In The World, the strip runs south for no more than half a mile. Even in that short stretch the gambling dens are interspersed with homely little motels, small stores and a Woolworths that still has a lunch counter. The street is narrow, clean and quiet, making Reno seem like that rare thing, an American small town that didn't die. It has no empty lots, no thrift stores, no doughnut development sucking the jam out of downtown.

It was divorce that put Reno on the map. From the turn of the century the rich and famous flocked to Reno, spending freely during the six months needed then to establish residency and so qualify for a divorce. And as the residency requirement was dropped, to three months in 1927 and six weeks in 1931, the business boomed. They called it taking the six-week cure. The daily train in became known as the divorcee special and newspaper society pages covered the comings and goings of the unhappily married, making Reno world-famous. It was while Arthur Miller was here in 1956, awaiting his divorce so that he could marry Marilyn, that he first conceived *The Misfits*.

Michelle told me she had wanted to be an actress. 'I've been in a couple of double Grade B movies,' she said, 'T and A movies to the nth degree. *Bikini Girl Beach Bunnies from Space* was one. That was in 1965. Girl invaders from Venus were going to take over the earth, and they landed in the desert. Their spaceship broke down near a dude ranch and they took over the ranch, killed all the guys then decided they needed to be by the ocean, which was where the bikinis came in. Then I came down to earth with bodyguards, I was the Spaced Queen. Not Space Queen, Spaced. Then there was *Teenage Vampettes*, and another called *Daughter of the Nile*.'

'They sound a bit Warhol-ish,' I said, thinking of the films he made in New York in the Sixties with transvestites such as Candy Darling. Michelle looked suspicious. 'Can you relate to Candy Darling?' I asked, thinking the question might spur a confession.

'I don't know about her,' she said in a change-the-subject tone. 'I don't know about all of those people,' then she dabbed at her nose, muttering about this summer cold that was threatening to lay her low. 'It's dropped my voice a whole octave,' she said.

These days, Michelle is a secretary for Reno social services, spending her time typing up social workers' reports. But, she said, the people she worked with were ants, she was a grasshopper. Under the name of Michelle Crystal she has a cabaret act in which she plays flamenco guitar and sings songs from Marilyn's movies. She never expressly says she is appearing as

Marilyn, she told me, but that was the general idea, and she felt audiences would get the message. I bet they did, though it may not have been the one she thought she was putting across.

Fifty miles through the desert north of Reno is Pyramid Lake, where Arthur Miller was holed up while he took his six-week cure. Much of *The Misfits* was filmed around here, particularly at the Stix Ranch in Quail Canyon by the lake shore.

We drove there up a dead straight two-lane blacktop, through sandy valleys hemmed in by barren hills where the only colour is in the names — Pah Rah Range, Hungry Valley and Dogskin Mountain. But then, after an hour's monotonous driving we rounded a bend, crested a rise and found an amazing sight before us. Pyramid Lake, a vast expanse of cool, clear water, had appeared in the middle of all this arid land. The waters were a rich blue, softened by the intensity of the sunlight to a distant hazy silver. There were mountains on the far shore, of such delicate hues that they appeared as if shaded in a hundred different tones of brown and sand and grey. There was hardly a feather of cloud in the sky, barely a ripple on the lake, just a narrow wet strip where the cool water touched the dark sand. It was a place of desolate, treeless beauty. We walked down to the water's edge.

The pyramid-shaped rock which gave the lake its name rose from the depths towards the far shore. There wasn't a house, a motel, a restaurant, or even a car park to be seen on the shoreline. Just south of the pyramid lay Large Anaho Island on which the American white pelican breeds. A couple passed overhead as we stood on the shore, stunning with their 10-foot wingspan, creamy white feathers and bright orange bills. For centuries the birds have bred here, migrating from Southern California and western Mexico. Because they have such sensitive nesting instincts they are seen as a measure of the wildness of such wilderness country as this. Predictably, their numbers have been declining in recent years, almost to the point of their disappearance.

The lake is another remnant, like Walker Lake which I had passed yesterday, of the giant prehistoric Lake Lahontan, discovered by the white man in 1844. Roslyn and Gay come swimming here in the movie, Michelle reminded me, in the scene where you realize they have become more than friends.

The place had Michelle thinking of Marilyn's death.

'I was in Hawaii, where I grew up, when I heard the news,' she said. 'I was swimming. Some friends told me, and I got really distraught. I felt like just swimming right out into the ocean. Screw everything. Who cares.'

She dabbed at her nose with a tissue which was full of holes.

'I never believed she had committed suicide. I got the idea that she had been taken away from us, from me, and that was really hard to cope with. And then, right after I heard Marilyn was dead, I started to feel that she was *in* me. There were no spirits, no communicating, no ouija board stuff. I just felt, again, like I had at the house in Reno, that she was saying to me "take it easy". So I didn't swim out.'

Uh huh? Let me get this straight. Marilyn is *in* Michelle?

Yes, she said, that's what it felt like.

'It was her presence, not talking to me or anything like that, but a feeling as if she was coming inside of me as she died. As she left her own, earthly body she was taking me over. And from then on I just started doing things in a small way that were her. The look, the make-up, hair; all that stuff.'

I took an appraising glance at her. She had a way to go on *that* front. You might be Marilyn on the inside, honey, but it sure ain't percolated through to the outside yet.

Michelle was in full confessional flow.

'I've had experiences in life that have made me feel that I truly am Marilyn,' she said. 'Without wanting to seem silly or superstitious. I mean, there is no reincarnation, or anything like that,' and she gave a little 'tee hee' girly giggle, 'but there have been some times in my life when we've seemed really close.

'I used to question it. I would do things and wonder why am I doing this, what is the reason? Maybe I'm just doing things that she didn't do, that she never had a chance to do. Oh God, I thought, this is crazy stuff, but the feeling persisted and I realized that, yes, with my life I was doing things she would want to do if she was free and had lived. Things she was too restricted to do because of her career, the things fame got in the way of her doing. Travel is a main one. I have travelled extensively. Marilyn wanted to travel and she couldn't.'

When Michelle went to Egypt to see the pyramids, I learned, Marilyn saw them too. Through Michelle, Marilyn had seen Japan, Africa, India, Europe. 'I've travelled all over for years.'

And now Michelle was back in Reno for two reasons. One was that her mother was here. She was in a nursing home, would not live long, and Michelle wanted to be around for her final years. But the other, she said, was because she felt closest to Marilyn in Reno, and the locations around it in which *The Misfits* was filmed.

On the way back to town we stopped to look at the horses in the Palomino Wild Horse and Burro Placement Center. Unlike the pelicans, the wild horses have been thriving in the thirty years since *The Misfits* was made. Then, the cowboys had trouble rounding up a handful to sell to the dogfood manufacturers. Today there are 30,000 roaming free in Nevada. But the optimum number is just 10,000.

So what do they do? They round them up and bring them to places like this. From here the young ones, which can be domesticated, become pets and the older ones are shipped to areas where there is no overcrowding. There were over a hundred horses in six large corrals, all marked with an orange N. I whistled to them but they would not come to the rails.

In the afternoon we drove to another *Misfits* location, south-east of Reno. Dayton was the setting for an important sequence in the movie involving a bar and a rodeo ground. The town is a forgotten little T-junction of a place just off the main highway. It looks like a movie set, with its Western buildings, few of which seemed to perform the functions that their painted signs would suggest for them. The Indian Motorcycles stores did not sell motorbikes, and the Fox Hotel, which had a sign offering board and lodging, was padlocked. A fat old dog and a man in a cowboy hat were asleep on a collapsing sofa under the porch. Opposite them, beyond a long empty plot, was the Odeon Hall Saloon.

The long, dark-wood bar was very much as I remembered it from the film. I recalled the scene in which Marilyn is playing a vigorous game of paddle ball while the drinkers gather round to watch the marvel of her swinging arse. The place is now called Mia's Swiss Restaurant, and EU and Swiss flags accompany the Stars and Stripes outside. In mid-afternoon, we were the only drinkers.

Mia, with an accent that made her sound as if she had never left Switzerland, served us with a beer and a Bloody Mary and filled us in on the history of the place. 'Ve renovated the whole thing,' she said. 'It vas closed years. It vas in a mess. It vas builded 1863 by the Chinese, they vas slave verkers or vatever, they had the mining, then it died. Now it's growing again because over the river ve haf a golf-course real-estate development. Arnold Palmer. About 500 new homes. But this town! The people! I don't know, could make a nice tourist thing if they vould clean up a little and not have all that chunk around.'

What about *The Misfits*? Sure, it brought a few people in. 'Ve haf posters for sale. You vant to buy?' No, we didn't want to buy, not even the one with Clark Gable giving Marilyn a fatherly hug.

Michelle had a theory about Clark Gable. It was quite possible he was Marilyn's father, she told me, though she did not exactly make a watertight case. Her idea was based on the simple fact that he was around at the right time and Marilyn's mother was in his circle. 'You have to remember,' she went on, 'Clark Gable was one of the most promiscuous men who ever lived. He was the Warren Beatty of his time.'

We drove back through Dayton and up into the hills to Virginia City. It clings halfway up the side of Mount Davidson like a Wild West town transported to Tuscany, a weird mix of a medieval Italian hill village and cowboy America. The cast had come to the Bucket of Blood saloon during breaks in shooting, I learned. Michelle asked the barmaid about the bar's name and we were told that once there had been a gambling room upstairs. One night a disagreement turned into a shoot-out. Blood ran between the floorboards and dripped into the buckets on the bar in which the beer was stored.

In the 1860s this was a true boom town. The very blue-grey mud that it is built on proved to be silver ore worth over $2,000 a ton. This now tiny, touristy place was once the most important settlement between Denver and San Francisco, and the men who arrived penniless to try their luck at prospecting were almost instantly transformed into millionaires, able to build mansions which they filled with the finest furnishings and fabrics from Europe and the Orient. Why, there was even a six-storey hotel which had the first elevator in the whole of the West.

At the rear of the bar, a picture window gave a spectacular view down Six Mile Canyon and over the parched hills to the mountains, shimmering in a haze on the horizon. Michelle went off to the ladies' room.

When she returned I went to the men's, but on the way I took a peek around the door of the ladies' to check whether she had left the seat up. She hadn't.

Higher up the hillside was a place called Edith Palmer's Country Inn. Marilyn had discovered it one day, stopping to look at its flower- and herb-filled garden, said Michelle. She had asked Edith Palmer for a packed lunch, which she made her, and returned regularly to the place she once described as her oasis in the desert. One night the whole film crew attended a birthday dinner here for one of the make-up men. A week later it was Arthur Miller's 45th birthday, the last social occasion of Marilyn's life with him. When asked in front of all the guests to stand up and say happy birthday to him she shook her head.

A man came towards us across the Inn's pretty cottage garden. Could we eat here? we asked. Well, no, he said, they were remodelling and were strictly bed and breakfast. What, even for a woman who has Marilyn Monroe inside her? Where was this guy's sense of history?

He directed us back down the street to a place called the Comstock, named after Henry Comstock, who also gave his name to the giant lode discovered here. Upstairs in the Victorian building was a cavernous room which doubled as cocktail bar and restaurant. The barman roused himself from the baseball game he was watching on a huge TV to show us to a table. There was a little dance floor, and a stage on which drums, organ and other instruments stood under wraps. A sign on the organ read Smitty the Montana Troubadour. Smitty was absent, fortunately.

The waiter was a boy with a weedy moustache and a little leather switch hanging from his belt. When Michelle dithered over the menu he took out the switch and made as if to chastise her with it. She giggled a great deal. Later, when she had pushed most of her vegetables to the side of her plate, he said, 'We have ways of making you eat your vegetables,' and pulled out a pair of handcuffs. Michelle giggled a great deal more. I had a nasty feeling that later on he would turn out to be Smitty, and serenade us.

The Carpenters were burbling away on the muzak tape playing in the background. I made a joke about them and shouldn't have. They turned out to be Michelle's favourite songwriters.

'I once wrote a song about Marilyn,' she said. 'It's kind of neat, I think. But I had to stop myself writing about her because I was identifying with her too much, it was like singing about myself. I felt stupid doing it. It was pretty though. The opening words were: "Marilyn, Marilyn you are the centre of my soul," stuff like that. That really is what I feel, but it was too intimate, too personal.'

Yes, I thought, it must have been a catchy little number.

Michelle was big on Marilyn's appeal, too. I was putting forward my theory that, really, Marilyn's fame had nothing to do with her abilities as an actress, that it was much more fundamental than that. People were attracted to what they saw as the essence of her.

'If you go far enough back to when people worshipped gods and goddesses you have the answer to the appeal of people like Marilyn,' said Michelle. 'The big film stars take on the functions of ancient gods and goddesses. People see them almost in a religious sense. And when they die young they are young for ever, they have immortality.

'Marilyn is the immortal goddess of love, and because of the cinema, because they have seen her in huge close-up, looking right at them, talking right to them, everyone feels they have had an intimate knowledge of her. And then, when you have Marilyn linked with John Kennedy, who was the hero type, the archetypal leader, you have the mating of gods and goddesses.'

As we drove back to Reno there was one final area I tried to probe. Michelle had told me that she had an older brother, called Michael, whom she was very close to during childhood. When they left home they had often travelled together. Both played flamenco guitar, but it was he who was sent to Spain to study the instrument while she lost out.

It seemed a little odd to have a brother and sister with such similar names. I asked if she was still close to him.

'He passed away. Heart problems. Three and a half years ago.'

Just a theory, but I wondered if Michelle had been born and grown up as Michael, transforming herself three years ago, after he died and when she came back to Reno to live. Just a theory.

As we said goodbye in Reno, Michelle offered her cheek for me to kiss. I moved gingerly in, hoping to give her a quick peck and get the hell on out of there, but when I got close she grabbed me in a hug. I tensed up and she let go. As I walked off I was wondering: those breasts . . . they had felt pretty hard. Could they be real?

I was still wondering as I boarded my plane for Memphis, and the Elvis death-fest. As I flew south I used Elvis to get Marilyn – and Michelle – out of my mind. But to do so was to go from the bizarre to the ridiculous. I leafed through the cuttings I had amassed about the followers of the King. Strange stories had not been hard to come across. There was the report about the Presley Commission who had published the results of a three-year-long investigation into the circumstances surrounding his death. This self-appointed team of twenty-five fans had concluded that Elvis had been forced to fake his death because of death threats from the Mafia, who had targeted him when President Nixon made him an honorary special agent for government drug-busters. To protect the King, the FBI gave him a new identity. Phil Aitcheson, a Memphis businessman and founder of the commission, said: 'This guy is such a master of disguise, you wouldn't even recognize him if he was living next door to you.'

I began thinking about my neighbour back home, a reclusive chap who appeared to use only one or two rooms in his house and spent the weekends tinkering with mysterious machines in his lean-to. Hmmm. Perhaps I should have been looking for Elvis rather closer to home.

Then there was the story about Elvis fan Eunice Fitch, who said she was brought back from a coma by the King appearing in a vision. Eunice, from Cannock in Staffordshire, who collapsed on the anniversary of Elvis's death, was played tapes of his music in hospital. Finally, after three days, she awoke and said: 'I have been with Elvis.' Presley, it seemed, had appeared at her bedside and promised she would recover.

Another story was about Peter Lovesey, who had been struck dumb by a stroke. For seven months he could not say a word. Then, one night at a karaoke evening in his local, the Plume of Feathers, Peter suddenly got up and sang 'Love Me Tender'. 'It's a miracle,' he said afterwards. 'The King has helped me speak again.'

Such tales seemed to crop up in the tabloids at the rate of about one a week.

There was the story of Alice Crader, a fifty-three-year-old from Jackson, Mississippi, who has not spoken a word since Elvis's death. She has vowed to stay silent until she is given concrete proof that the King is dead.

In Oldbury, West Midlands, a thirty-six-year-old bachelor called Dennis Taylor died after spending eighteen days in bed listening to Elvis records. He took to his bed after a girlfriend left him, and died from a blood clot in his leg caused by his inactivity. He had been obsessed with Elvis since the age of eight.

There was only one word for all this, and that word was 'sad'. But things would get sadder in Memphis.

CHAPTER FOUR

Disgraceland

ELVIS PRESLEY, MEMPHIS, TENNESSEE, 16 AUGUST

'I imagine that I discover Elvis had some sperm put in a sperm bank just before his death. No-one knows about this but me. He tells me in a dream or something. He says go there, tell them Elvis sent you, and they will understand. So I go to the sperm bank and tell them, and I am impregnated with Elvis's sperm. And I get pregnant and it is a boy and I bring him up to know he is Elvis's son and heir. Not that I want to make a claim on the estate or anything, but I want him to know who his father was, what happened to him, where things went wrong, and to avoid all the pitfalls that Elvis fell into. And the wonderful thing for me is that having Elvis's child as my son is like having Elvis always with me.' This was Debra talking.

'I guess the fantasy fulfils two things. For one, I get as close to Elvis as I can without actually having him in my arms, the other is that I can save his son from the things that destroyed his father.'

In the Elvis calendar, 8 January, his birthday, is Christmas and 16 August, the anniversary of his death, is Easter. So it was Easter in Memphis, and the followers had come to his shrine, Graceland, the mansion that sits on a six-lane highway on the southern fringes of the city. I was among tens of thousands of visitors who had come for the Death Week celebrations, the lookalike contests at a diner called Bad Bob's Vapours where they might see young Elvises, old Elvises, a female Elvis, a Mexican and a black Elvis, even a child Elvis, all blasting out 'American Trilogy' and 'My Way'. They had come to tour Graceland, maybe take a side trip out to his birthplace in Tupelo, down in Mississippi, and talk and talk and talk Elvis with other true believers. The highlight of their trip would be the candle-lit procession, on the night of 15–16 August, through the gates of Graceland, up the winding path to the memorial garden where Elvis is buried, to pay their respects. As Muslims go to Mecca and Catholics to Lourdes, Elvis fans come to Memphis and to Graceland.

The whole of Memphis seemed to be in expectation. The fans had come from all over the States and around the world. The motels were full, particularly the ones along Elvis Presley Boulevard, on which Graceland sits. I had been really lucky to get a plane ticket, and a motel room, at such short notice. Or so everybody told me.

But listening to Debra's Elvis fantasy was not a part of the official tour. And this was not Graceland. This was Disgraceland. I was feeling enormously privileged to be eavesdropping on some real, hardcore, Elvis girls'-talk. There was more to come.

'My fantasy's a whole lot simpler. I just want to get laid by him,' said an uncomplicated soul called Lisa.

'Young Elvis or old Elvis?' she was asked.

'Oh purleese! Young Elvis. I want to see if that pelvis moves like that in the sack.'

There were squeals. Lisa turned to me. 'Know who Little Elvis was?'

I said I did not.

'That was Elvis's pet name for his wiener. I'd like to adopt Little Elvis, take him home and raise him like he was my own.'

Clare was more lyrical. 'I think of Elvis aged sixty-five, old and frail and sitting in an armchair in my parents' house, the house I grew up in,' she said. 'And he is my grandfather, but he is also Elvis. And I'm a little girl and I get to sit on his knee and talk to him. My parents don't know he is Elvis, that is his and my secret. And when they are away in other parts of the house he will sing me a song, really low, like 'Love Me Tender' or something. Sing it just for me. I know the time-scale is all messed up in this, but it is like he didn't die but had to escape and only I know who he used to be.'

It was early evening. The exact moment of Elvis's passing is unknown, but was probably around ten o'clock on the morning of the 16th. He was sitting on the toilet when the years of abusing prescription drugs and gorging on junk food finally caught up with him. But, maybe because Elvis was such a night-time person, going to bed at dawn and rising in the afternoon, it is at night that the ceremonies take place.

Tonight the focus would be on Graceland, and later I would be going there, to join the procession past the grave, but first I wanted to enjoy Disgraceland. It was not a club, not a fan club in the formal sense, just a group of mainly single, twentysomething and thirtysomething Memphis women who loved Elvis but had an unconventional way of showing it. They were meeting in a suburban bungalow in Memphis. In the spacious lounge a dozen women lazed around, sipping wine, talking and joking, as if it were an over-age slumber party.

'A lot of fans are real reverential to Elvis,' explained Josie, whose house this was, 'but we are a disgrace to his name.' There was a chorus of laughter.

'And we're proud of it,' said another voice.

'You betcha.'

'That's because the official side of Elvis is so tacky it has driven away his true fans,' went on Josie. 'I mean, come on. How can anybody who has any taste at all buy any of the Elvis souvenirs, or go round Graceland without throwing up? Elvis was hijacked during his life by a manager who made him do trashy films and squander his talent, and by so-called friends and minders who let him drug himself to death. After his death he has been hijacked by fans with no taste and no style. Think of Elvis in 1958, so cool, so well-dressed, so beautiful, so sexy . . .'

'Hey stop that will you, you'll get me goin' again!'

'. . . So we like to sit around, watch videos which people bring along, listen to his records, drink plenty of wine or beer, and eat cheeseburgers and banana splits. You know about his eating habits, right? Well Elvis's staple diet, they say, in his final days, was cheeseburgers and banana splits. He would eat three of each at a time,' Josie concluded.

The women said they meant no disrespect to Elvis. 'Well,' Debra explained, 'we are disrespectful to mainstream Elvis worshippers. That's a fact. What they do sucks. But we have nothing but respect for him. It's not that we don't think his decline was a tragedy, which it was. I guess it's just that we have different ways of showing it. I guess it helps us to laugh at it.'

And then there was a chorus of 'Shut up!' They don't like to rationalize, they just want to have fun. To fantasize, and tell Elvis stories. Rae had one:

'When I was a little girl I had an Elvis dressing-up set,' she said. 'There was a cardboard Elvis and a set of outfits. The Elvis was dressed in just his underwear, a white undershirt with short sleeves and a pair of white boxers. I remember my friends used to come round and we'd go in my bedroom and take off one outfit and put on another. But when they weren't there I used to take his clothes off and hug him. Once I slipped him inside my pyjama bottoms. (Raucous laughter.) 'But then I whipped him out again and was terrified at what I had done.'

'You thought you were going to get pregnant?'

'I don't think I knew what I was doing at all, I guess I was just following an instinct. But afterwards I was so ashamed. I threw away the doll and the clothes. My mother saw them in the trash can and asked why

I had got rid of them – I guess because they had been about my most precious toy for weeks before that. I just said I was tired of Elvis and she was relieved. I remember overhearing her telling my father. They thought it was healthy that I had got rid of a little-girl obsession. Little did they know!'

And this was how the evening went on at Disgraceland. It was a lot of fun, but I was off to Graceland itself. Pop back if you get bored with all that reverential shit, they said. Thanks, I said, I would.

I had been two days in Memphis, a city I had visited before and of which I had fond memories. And I had expected it to be pure delight, here at the height of the Elvis calendar. But this time around it seemed like the ugliest of places, populated by the ugliest of people. They could be delegates of the Fat Arse Convention of America. You have never seen such butts in such number. These backsides started beneath the armpit and ended at the knee. They caused gridlock everywhere in the city. Every door to every fast-food restaurant in Memphis had one wedged in it. Firemen were cutting fat arses out of their cars at every intersection. There wasn't a lavatory in the place that didn't have one stuck to it by suction.

I mean, I love Elvis. But the question has to be asked. If Elvis was so great, why are his fans so ugly?

Downtown Memphis was a place of history and dignity – as I remembered it. It is the place which gave birth to the blues – commemorated in the renovated historic area of Beale Street – and to rock and roll for which we have Elvis to thank. Sun Studios, where he made his first recordings, is restored, reopened and functioning both as a tourist attraction and a recording studio. The Lorraine Motel, where the black civil-rights campaigner Martin Luther King was assassinated in 1968, has been reborn as the National Civil Rights Museum. Downtown, to my recollection, was a cool and civilized place. But as Elvis's big day approached, it was filling up with every aimlessly wandering freak in America. Every overweight man seemed to think he would be a dead ringer for Elvis if he wore a pair of heavy shades and left his shirt unbuttoned.

It was only because of my mood of despair that, the day before, I had allowed myself to be hijacked by a couple of English Elvis fans. They were a middle-aged couple, Harry and Vi, from Yorkshire. You could spot Harry for an English tourist a mile off – he wore shorts, a pale blue beany hat, a camcorder, and black socks under his open-toed sandals. We got talking and when they discovered I was English and alone they insisted on adopting me for the afternoon. Harry held out a horny hand and said, 'Take the hand of the man that once took the hand of the man you love.' This meant, it turned out later, that Harry had once shaken hands with Elvis – from the front row of a concert in Vegas – and wanted to do me the honour of letting me touch the hand that shook Elvis's.

In Memphis they were being looked after, they told me, by Vi's cousin Dorothy. They were waiting for her now. She had gone to get the car and then they were going out to eat. I must come with them! In the ten minutes we waited they gave me Dorothy's life story. She had married a US serviceman and moved with him to Memphis right after the Second World War. But she was widowed nearly ten years before and now she lived for Elvis.

A car pulled up and Harry said to Dorothy, 'We've met up with this English lad and he's coming with us for some grub, all right?' We were off.

'She's had us all over the show,' said Harry to me quietly as we sat in the back of the car, the women up front. 'We're knackered. We've been out to Tupelo, seen the birth site, the little wooden house he lived in, seen where he bought his first guitar, come down here, been round Graceland, seen the lookalike show at Bad Bob's, been round the museum, been on both his planes, seen his car collection – now that were good.'

They were staying at Wilson World, a pink palace across the street from Graceland. They were very disappointed they couldn't get in at the place down the street which had twenty-four-hour Elvis movies in the rooms. That was their fault, Dorothy chipped in. If they had told her earlier they were coming she could have booked them in, but they had to go and put it off and put it off. Harry grimaced behind her.

We were headed for a place called the Western Steak House and Lounge at 1298 Madison, in a middling district east of downtown. Dorothy was saying this was not on the usual tourists' itinerary. This was something only the locals could show you. It was Elvis's favourite restaurant, the place he used so regularly when he first became famous that they reserved the corner booth for him and it was christened Elvis's Booth.

'Sizzling steaks anytime,' said a sign.

'You go right in and you ask to sit in Elvis's Booth,' Dorothy said as she bustled into the restaurant, us hurrying to keep up with her. They hummed and hawed because it was booked for later in the evening but Dorothy persisted, said it was only five and we'd be real fast, and they let us. It felt like a great triumph until we got inside and found the place – a gloomy, dark-wood affair – was absolutely empty. There was a cutting on the wall of an interview with Lil Thomsen, owner of the steak house, in which she reminisced about Elvis in his early days, when he was a country boy in an old shirt – not good-looking at all – and came to like this booth diagonally opposite the door in which he could sit with his back to the wall and see everyone coming and going.

So how were they enjoying Memphis, I asked Harry and Vi after Dorothy had bustled off to the ladies' room and we were looking through the menu. Actually, they said, Dorothy took all this Elvis stuff a bit seriously. They liked him of course, always had, always would, but she went a bit far.

82

'I think it's a religion with her,' said Harry, to a frown from Vi. 'It is,' he insisted, 'she talks as if Elvis were Jesus Christ hisself.'

All of a sudden this sounded promising. I perked up a little. And when Dorothy came back I asked her about it and they flashed me a look that said 'Now you've done it. There'll be no stopping her now.'

Dorothy looked at me warily, her suspicion of me momentarily outweighing her desire to spread the word about Elvis.

'A lot of folk poke fun,' she said in a voice that was three-quarters Tennessee, a quarter Bradford. 'But when you study Elvis's life like I have, you see that there are so many parallels between his life and the life of Jesus.'

So I asked her if she thought Elvis *was* Jesus, as some fans seemed to. She was affronted at the suggestion.

'No,' she said, 'they were like partners, like two sides of the same coin. Elvis wasn't Jesus, but he was the same as him in a lot of ways. Elvis and Jesus were both messengers from God. But don't forget what Elvis said, when people called him the King. He said there was only one King, and that is Jesus Christ.'

But, she went on, the evidence of Elvis's special status was all there. The clues were there for believers to read. I asked for a for-instance.

'For instance,' she answered, 'take the phrase Jesus lives. Well, Elvis is an anagram for lives. So you have in the phrase Jesus lives, the names Jesus and Elvis. The Lord put Elvis alongside Jesus. Elvis knew that, he came to know he had a mission.'

The waitress was there saying, 'Can I get you folks something to drink?' and Harry was making his little joke, asking, 'Have ye got a pint of Tetleys?'

'No sir we do not, we have Coors, Coors Lite, Miller, Miller Lite, Miller Original Draught, Bud, Bud Lite, Bud Dry . . .' and on and on for ever.

'Elvis was a twin,' Dorothy continued. 'The first twin born was Jesse Garon, who was born dead. When Elvis was born there was a mystic blue light shining over Tupelo as there was the star of Bethlehem when Christ was born, to guide folks to him. Jesus was born in a stable.'

'But Elvis wasn't,' I said, thankful of some small detail I felt confident in challenging her on. I knew he was born in a little two-room shack.

'Have you seen that shack?'

I had.

'Why, it ain't much better than a stable.'

Nor was Graceland, in my opinion, unless you think being able to watch three TVs at once will raise your quality of life.

'She's going to get her Bible out,' said Harry.

Dorothy got her Bible out. 'When I read the story of Jesus it's like I'm also reading the story of Elvis,' she said. 'Now I'm not saying I don't have to interpret things a little, but that's the way the Bible is supposed to be.'

She prepared to read, saying, 'This is right after Herod has asked the wise men where he can find Jesus.'

'"After they had left, the angel of the Lord appeared to Joseph in a dream and said, 'Get up, take the child and his mother with you, and escape into Egypt, and stay there until I tell you, because Herod intends to search for the child and do away with him.'"'

'Now, the Presleys were driven out of Tupelo. They were given two days to leave. And they had to flee Mississippi and cross the state line into Tennessee, just like Mary and Joseph had to take their son Jesus from Israel into Egypt.

'You see, Vernon, Elvis's dad, he had been driven on to the wrong side of the law on occasions to provide for his family in times of need. He had served time for a cheque forgery, and he was in a whole lot of trouble again.'

And did the Mississippi Herod kill all the boys who were two or under, I wondered. No matter. The point was, Dorothy clearly believed all this.

She was flipping on through her Bible, saying, 'Now, Jesus had his people around him, his twelve disciples, Elvis had his guys. And those guys were as dedicated to Elvis as the disciples were to Jesus. When Jesus spoke he gathered thousands of people before him. Everywhere he went they came to listen to him. That's so true of Elvis, and not just when he was performing. All the time he was at home in Graceland there were hundreds of people waiting outside, wanting to get to see him or touch him.'

The waitress came with four red plastic gingham napkins, all-enveloping ones that covered us from neck to lap, and which she fastened behind on each of us. It was like being dressed for dinner as a kid. Harry was chuckling. 'D'ye think I'm a messy eater or what?' We looked really stupid. Especially Dorothy, Bible in her hand, like an evangelist for carnivorism. She talked right through this operation, too, of how Jesus had had his time in the wilderness, his time of doubt and so, Lord knows, had Elvis. 'The devil tempted Elvis more than he could just about anybody else because Elvis had the means to sin. The devil showed him that he could have anything, any person, if he wanted. Elvis did fall into temptation.

'And I believe Elvis found all the money and the fame and the adulation to be very confusing. After all, to be from the humble background that he was from and to find yourself almost like the chosen one, and have adoring crowds around you all the time, hanging on your every word as they hung on every word of Jesus . . . it ain't easy to come to terms with.'

She said that Elvis had had a vision in the desert, just as Jesus did. It was in Arizona. 'He saw the face of Stalin, and when he looked it turned into the face of Jesus. It was the antichrist turning into Christ, and Elvis took that to be a sign that he had to be good and to do good.'

Then the sizzling steaks arrived. And boy did they sizzle. They were on cast-iron skillets, mine and

Harry's big things hanging over the edges, running in blood and juices and hissing like mad on the hot metal.

'That's summat like,' said Harry.

'And Elvis did something very like Jesus rising from the dead,' Dorothy picked up when we had all taken a mouthful. 'He did it in 1968, when he was thirty-three, the same age as Jesus when he rose from the dead. 'Cept Elvis rose through television, which Jesus would have used if he had had it at his disposal. He did a TV show, they called it the comeback show because he had been away so long, shut up in Graceland or in Hollywood, or wherever. It went out on satellite all over the world.'

I asked her about the dark side of Elvis. What about the over-indulgence in drugs and food, the money he spent, the rich lifestyle? There was an explanation for that, said Dorothy. 'Elvis had God and the Devil battling inside of him. It's like half of him was God-fearing, loved his country, loved his mother, but there was another side that was bad. And that evil side came from his dead twin, Jesse. Cos when Jesse Garon died, his soul went into Elvis. It was Jesse Garon who liked the guns, the girls, the cursing. Elvis and Jesse were in a struggle for Elvis's earthly body, and in the end Jesse got it. The Devil had Elvis's body so he had to escape.

'He knew his time had truly come as well. He knew he was going to die. He warned his companions, like Christ had done. He foretold the day of his death too. He gave us a sign that he was to die, it was right there in the music that started his live shows. Anyone could have seen the sign if they had an eye and a mind to. I confess that I did not understand it until it was brought to my attention after he died.'

I was puzzled. Go on, what was it?

'It was in the music that opened his show. The music was from the movie *2001*. And if you look at the date of his death, which was 16.8.1977, and add those numbers up, what number do you get?'

I did a quick calculation.

'2001.'

'Right. Elvis was betrayed by his friends. Peter denied his Lord and Judas sold him for thirty pieces of silver. Elvis was betrayed by three of the guys who were closest to him and who were supposed to look out for him. They wrote a book, a shameful book, which was full of the worst kind of tales, about drugs and about how overweight Elvis had become, and how he was like a baby, not able to control his bodily functions.'

She was referring to a book called *Elvis: What Happened?* which was written just before Elvis's death by three former employees – Red and Sonny West and Dave Hebler. I had often heard this cited by fans as a traitorous act and one of the things that killed him.

'They crucified him in print,' said Dorothy. 'It was a real Judas act, selling Elvis for thirty pieces of silver. You know, Elvis only lived three weeks after that book came out.'

'A-men to that,' said Harry, looking up momentarily from his plate, where the blood flowed.

There were thousands of people milling around the gates of Graceland at 9 p.m. on 15 August. There was an expectant hum of conversation as the preparations for the vigil were completed. The presidents of the many dozens of Elvis fan clubs lined the curving driveway that rises up the hill to the steps of the mansion, then off to the side and the memorial garden.

We waited while a light was taken from the eternal flame on Elvis's grave. Then two huge candles bearing Elvis's light were brought to the foot of the drive and the fans passed through, each lighting their own candle, so that the lights from Elvis's grave multiplied and multiplied. Then, slowly, to the sound of Elvis's music relayed over the hot night air, the multitude shuffled up the hill and round to the memorial garden, where Elvis, his father, mother and grandmother are buried. And there they paused, by the graves, the memorial to Jesse Garon, Elvis's twin, beneath the statue of Christ flanked by two angels which has carved on it IHS at the top, Presley at the bottom. Many cried, some spoke, some were clearly praying, others bending to read the notes on the bunches of flowers in a multi-coloured mound which completely covered Elvis's grave.

And the question that kept occurring to me was what on earth was I doing there? My predicament reminded me of the scene in Woody Allen's *Everything You Wanted To Know About Sex But Were Afraid To Ask*, where the little men dressed in white who play the massed sperm are ready to go over the top when suddenly a little black sperm comes into view, looking utterly bewildered and asking, 'How the hell did I get here?' I was that little black sperm. I couldn't even laugh at it any longer. The people I met at the graveside were a succession of saddies, deluded that their empty lives were filled by Elvis.

There was a woman called Kiki Apostolakos, who told me how the announcement of Elvis's death had come to her like a revelation, like a command that she must follow him. So she had divorced her husband in Greece, and married an American so that she could come to Memphis. When he died she dedicated her life to Elvis

'I come to the grave at dawn every single day,' she told me. 'I leave flowers, tidy the grave, and I pray. When I left Greece my parents went crazy. Why do you leave your home and your family for a dead man? You don't even know him.

'I could not explain, but I had to come. Then my husband he died, and ever since I have lived only for Elvis. I am dead to any other man, I could never have any man now. I am faithful to Elvis and I will love him for the rest of my life. But I am not lonely. I meet so many people through Elvis. I meet them at the grave, and they write to me, ask me to pray for them up here. So I am a kind of messenger to Elvis from his fans.'

I also met a woman called Cyndi Silvia, who had founded a fan club called Elvis Memphis Style. She told me that what looked like obsession in a fan could be misconstrued.

'I met a couple back in 1988 – don't ask me their names because I can't even remember them – but they used to spend six months in Florida and six months in Memphis. Every day while they were in Memphis they went up to his graveside. I'm thinking, This is bizarre. I go to speak with them. It turns out they had two kids who had cystic fibrosis in the sixties. Elvis paid hospital bills until they died. So in their small way they were just trying to thank him and repay him.'

She was crying as she told me this.

There seemed to be as many images of Elvis as there were fans who remembered him. Undeniably, he was one of the ultimate embodiments of the American Dream. He was the poor boy who became the greatest entertainer in the world. You could see him as a great singer, pure and simple, as a sex symbol, or even as a kitsch joke, and still enjoy him enormously.

But the most striking thing, I thought, as I watched the fat butts dripping candle wax over one another and waited for the first spontaneous combustion, was the way that so many of them spoke of him as if he were a saint, if not more. Even putting aside those to whom he was a Christ figure, many saw him as a truly admirable human being, as a person who, through his generosity, his acts of charity, deserved to be canonized. It was easy to see his story in a religious light. There were those who explained the myriad reported sightings of Elvis many years after his death as manifestations of a fervent wish for his resurrection.

But did they want him back to make some more records and play a few more seasons at Vegas? No, they did not. They wanted a saint to live. A man who showed what could be done – what they could do – whatever their disadvantages. They wanted a man who showed great reserves of goodness to continue his good works. As I had discovered with Marilyn Monroe, it was what was perceived as the true essence of the person beneath the fame, the success, the glamour, that attracted the most dedicated fans. It was this essence that they sought and which they wanted to remember.

Arise Saint Elvis.

My many conversations with Elvis and Marilyn obsessives were starting to take their toll. I felt like an overburdened doctor who begins to sense in himself all the symptoms of the many ailments he diagnoses in his patients.

And, you know, speaking as a medical practitioner, people often ask me: 'Doctor, when did the human race first contract this particular virus of hero-worship?' And, as a doctor, I tell them that, should we so desire, we will find the roots of this phenomenon back in Los Angeles, on 23 August. Please bear with me during a brief history lesson.

CHAPTER FIVE

The Lady in Black

RUDOLPH VALENTINO,
LOS ANGELES, CALIFORNIA, 23 AUGUST

I was looking for the Lady in Black. The problem was, which Lady in Black was I looking for?

I knew the story, that on the anniversary of Rudolph Valentino's death, 23 August, a lady in black would place flowers on his tomb in the Hollywood Memorial Park Cemetery.

So here I was, and here were the ladies in black. At least a dozen of them. Some of them were men dressed as ladies in black. One man in black was on the arm of a female Valentino lookalike. There were other lookalikes and generally camp individuals. It was a raucous scene as they jostled for position on the steps of the mausoleum in a corner of the spacious and peaceful cemetery.

It had felt like an oasis of calm when I turned off Santa Monica Boulevard into its green, palm-dotted acres, but in this corner the scene was anything but tranquil.

I moved around the group trying to spot an authentic-looking lady in black and when that failed I turned to the one or two people who were not playing a role and who turned out to be the less extreme Valentino fans. It was shrill, they agreed, but they had seen worse. There had been squabbles between those who considered themselves genuine mourners and others they accused of coming just to get their pictures in the papers. One

91

year an aspiring actress had marched in, along with a photographer, and begun relating how she was sleeping with Valentino's ghost. There have even been fights, I was told, with roses getting stomped underfoot.

But what of the real Lady in Black, I asked? They knew there used to be a Lady in Black, but didn't think she came along any more. Probably scared off by this crowd.

So I gave up and left. It was only by chance that I came back, several days later. And I'm very glad I did.

The Valentino story intrigued me because he was the first Strange Angel. The first star to receive mass posthumous adulation, the first to enter people's dreams and fantasies. He was the forerunner of James Dean, Marilyn Monroe and Elvis Presley.

And, without the Valentino crowd, the Hollywood Memorial Park Cemetery was a wonderful, time-locked place too. It harked back to Hollywood's – and Los Angeles's – golden age. Here I felt immune to the noise, the crime, the squalor. Here, among streets that did not even have the faded, low-rent fun of Hollywood Boulevard and Sunset, an area of mean houses, mean stores and borderline businesses, was a secret garden whose high walls protected it from L.A.'s ugly sprawl.

The winos might be shuffling past in the street outside, but they did not come in here. Almost no-one did. The sprinklers were keeping the grass a lush green beneath the palm trees as I cruised around Lakeview Avenue, and I could hear children at play in a neighbouring school. It was a perfect place to come and sit and take stock, to think about Marilyn and Elvis.

They had a great deal in common. They were stars from a lost era, from a time when the famous were untouchable deities. When they made contact with their fans it was as if they were bestowing a blessing and the fans were meek supplicants. But today stars are seen as ordinary people, no better or worse than average, with the same mundane problems about their careers, their marriages, their families.

Once the excesses of superstars, the over-indulgences in drink or drugs or sex, were seen as part of a charmed life, a life of heightened sensations and pleasures. Now they are seen as the weaknesses of inadequates who, when the constraints were off, did not know when to stop, like children let loose in a sweet shop.

And the nature of a fan's response to stars has changed too. Instead of seeing them as heroes, we are supposed to sympathize with them. It must be *so* tough having enough money to spend on drugs to enable you to kill yourself any day of the week. It must be *so* tough having so many women chasing you that you can't remain faithful and your marriage is wrecked. Thank God I'm a nonentity and saved from your own particular mink-lined little tragedy.

But Marilyn and Elvis are different. Despite the posthumous attempts to demystify them they still sparkle and shine, because they were of an era before stars were routinely brought to their knees. They remain heroes that their fans can look up to. And because they are so exalted, their problems, the minutiae of their lives, really matter. If some discredited star dies young today, who cares? Today they will be seen as spoilt boys or girls who somehow couldn't prevent themselves from fouling their beautiful nests.

Marilyn and Elvis did not die of excess. They both died of neglect. Marilyn, in a career that was one long crying-out to be loved, was a fragile bloom that should have been nurtured. There are all sorts of theories about how she came to overdose on barbiturates. But if we put aside the theories about an overdose administered, either accidentally or on purpose, by a third party, and assume she took the drug herself, she did so not to heighten her pleasure but to dull her pain. Elvis, despite surrounding himself with friends who were supposed to protect him – from himself and others – had his most dangerous appetites fatally indulged by these people.

This is why the fans I had met felt guilt at their heroes' passing. That was why Ruth wished she could have been Marilyn's friend, to support and protect her. It was why Cyndi Sylvia, the nurse whom I met at Elvis's grave, said, 'I should have been his private duty nurse. He would not have had to worry about anything then. Those around him, they would have had to go through me to get to him and I would have protected him. He would still be alive today if the nursing of him had been down to me.'

I was thinking about all this, wandering around the cemetery where Cecil B. De Mille has his Greek temple memorial and Douglas Fairbanks senior lies in a sunken garden at the end of a black oblong of water. Charlie Chaplin has a crypt here in the Abbey of the Psalms and John Huston, director of *The Misfits*, rests beneath the palm trees. And I wondered again about Valentino, and the Lady in Black. The Valentino story is a fascinating one, and it was sad to think it might have been snuffed out, turned into an annual circus side-show.

After Valentino's premature death, aged thirty-one, in 1926 – from complications that set in after he suffered a gastric ulcer and ruptured appendix – a cult developed comparable to the one that now surrounds Elvis, Marilyn or James Dean. Of all the stars in the early days of cinema, his appeal was the most intriguing. The characters he played, in just seven years as a star, pursue and capture women, treading a fine line between powerful seduction and rape.

It seems contradictory that a man playing such roles should be so hugely popular at a time when women were beginning to enjoy the fruits of emancipation that followed the First World War. But watching his films was a way of flaunting that emancipation. Being a Valentino fan went with smoking, drinking and wearing short skirts. Valentino came along at a time of sexual awakening, he brought previously undreamt-of possibilities, he was alien and exotic. Many men viewed him with disdain, but to millions of women he was the perfect lover they had always dreamed of: a modern-day Casanova.

Valentino's passion, however, seems to have been reserved for the screen. His first wife, an actress called Jean Acker, whom he married a matter of days after they met, locked the world's greatest lover out of their bedroom on their wedding night. Valentino and his second wife, Natacha Rambova, seemed to have little passion for each other. There has been speculation that neither marriage was consummated, that both women may have been lesbians, Valentino may have been gay.

But no-one is very interested in his life: it is Valentino's image that has held so many millions of women spellbound. And, though there is no evidence that Valentino was at all promiscuous, dozens of women appeared after his death claiming he had fathered their children. There were also numerous women who said Valentino had communicated with them in spirit messages. His second wife, Natacha, was among them. There were several suicides by women who hoped to join Rudi on the other side, one woman holding his portrait to her chest and shooting herself through the picture.

During his life he had received great attention from fans, employing two secretaries to handle the mail and send out 1,000 photographs a week. When he died, 100,000 filed past his coffin when he lay in state in New York. There were hourly radio bulletins about the nation's shock and grief. Two funeral ceremonies were held, the first in New York, where 12,000 lined the funeral route and 6,000 attended the service, the second in Los Angeles, where 5,000 paid their respects. On the coffin's journey by train across America, interest was such that 200 would turn out at a suburban station, despite the fact that strenuous efforts were made to keep the route and timing of the journey secret. The day after the funeral, 10,000 went to Hollywood Memorial Park.

It was in 1930, four years after his death, that a Lady in Black first appeared. A veil covered her face and she refused to say who she was or to answer any other questions. Soon other women began appearing, all keeping their identities secret. By the end of the decade a dozen attended the memorial services held at 12.10 each 23 August.

In 1937 it seemed that the mystery of the original lady in black was answered. Russell Birdwell, a film publicist, claimed to have paid a young unknown actress to appear as the Lady in Black to promote a film called *The Only Normal Man in Hollywood*. In this, a woman called the Lady in Black appears as a minor character. Several years after the film was completed, the Lady in Black was still appearing each 23 August and the *L.A. Herald Express* commissioned Birdwell to investigate and try to discover the woman's identity.

To his great surprise, he discovered that the Lady in Black was the same actress from the film, still wearing the outfit she wore on screen. He also discovered that a second woman was acting out the same fantasy. Birdwell revealed his secret, but his announcement attracted little interest. Valentino fans, it seemed, did not want explanations that shattered their illusions; they preferred to believe in the myth of the Lady in Black.

In 1939, three ladies in black appeared. The following year Valentino's first wife, Jean Acker, turned up, mourned silently and placed red roses before the tomb.

Also in 1940, a former Ziegfeld Follies performer, Marian E. Watson, claimed that she was the original Lady in Black, that she had secretly married Valentino in New Jersey the year before his death and had two children with him. In 1951, after several unsuccessful attempts on her life, she died from an overdose of sleeping pills.

In 1947 a long-serving but hitherto anonymous Lady in Black identified herself as Ditra Flame, said she had

Marilyn Monroe: her blonde, pouting image is reproduced endlessly as the ideal embodiment of feminine sexuality. *Hulton Deutsch Collection*

In Hollywood Boulevard, the souvenir shops are filled with items bearing Marilyn's image. She, Elvis and James Dean are like a tourist-tat Trinity. *Rex Features*

Inset: At Marilyn's modest grave. 'She was only the most famous woman in the world,' said my guide, 'you'd think they could make some effort.' *Rex Features*

Newspaper headlines: John Frost Historical Newspaper Service

VOL. LXXXI   SIX PARTS—PART ONE   MONDAY MORNING, AUGUST 6, 1962

MARILYN MONROE
1926 - 1962

MARILYN MO
FOUND DEAD
Sleeping Pill Overdose Blamed

Elvis Presley dies at 42

Heart attack was cause of his death

Elvis Presley: his resurrection is so ardently desired by many people that sightings of him are commonplace.
Rex Features

On the anniversary of his death, tens of thousands file past Elvis's garishly decorated grave in the grounds of Graceland, his Memphis home.
Rex Features

Loving Elvis is one thing, but becoming him is the fervent wish of the most obsessive look-alikes. *Rex Features*

VALENTINO IS DEAD!

DIES BRAVELY

RUDOLPH VALENTINO

Sheik Dies Nonchalantly Asking for More Sunlight

By JAMES L. KILGALLEN,
International News Service Staff Correspondent.

NEW YORK—Rudolph Valentino, idol of millions of motion picture fans throughout the world, died in Poly-clinic hospital at 12:10 this afternoon aft

Death came eight days

To the end he

GRAFT
FI

Rudolph Valentino: the first star to receive mass posthumous adulation; the forerunner to Marilyn, Elvis, Dean and Kennedy.
Popperfoto

The grave of the Lady in Black, who claimed to be Valentino's lover and whose daughter insists Valentino was her father. Daily she tends this and Valentino's grave.

Melly Meadows is the official Scarlett O'Hara of small-town Jonesboro, Georgia, where *Gone with the Wind* is set.

Rhett Butler look-alike David Spohn takes his fascination with the character so far that he has numerous props, including an American Express card in Butler's name.

James Dean is still the ultimate teenage rebel, with an image so potent that it can sell anything: savings accounts to British students, blank videotapes to the Japanese and Gap khaki trousers to the world.
Rex Features

Little Bastard, the Porsche in which James Dean died.
Rex Features

After the death of his mother, Dean was brought up in this Indiana farmhouse by his aunt and uncle. His cousin Marcus still lives here, and tolerates the fans.

A sign marks the way to Dean's final resting-place.

Dean's grave in Fairmount Cemetery is always covered with lipstick kisses.

On the anniversary of Dean's death, look-alikes visit the crash site and the nearby Dean memorial.

James Dean
2ND DRIVE ON RIGHT
TOP OF HIL

JAMES B. DEAN
1931 · 1955

River Phoenix was heralded as the new James Dean, but will his early death make him an enduring icon? *Rex Features*

Outside the Viper Room where Phoenix died, the fans leave their tributes and their graffiti: rivers flow into seas, phoenixes rise from the ashes. *Rex Features*

Ed Gein after his arrest. Though he was the model for murderers in *Psycho* and *The Silence of the Lambs*, his evil surpassed either fictional representation.
Range/Bettmann/UPI

At Ed Gein's farmhouse, police found a catalogue of horrors that were unique in their grotesqueness. *Range/Bettmann/UPI*

Bernice Worden was the blameless proprietor of Plainfield's hardware store, but Gein shot her in the shop and then butchered her like a deer. *Range/Bettmann/UPI*

Gein robbed dozens of graves in Plainfield Cemetery and crafted hideous trophies from the female body parts he stole. *Range/Bettmann/UPI*

KENNEDY SLAIN
ON DALLAS STREET

★ ★ ★ ★   ★ ★ ★ ★   ★ ★ ★ ★   ★ ★ ★ ★

John F. Kennedy and his wife Jacqueline: the image of what America lost. *Rex Features*

Every day hundreds of people flock to Dealey Plaza in Dallas, where Kennedy was shot, to try and decide for themselves whether Lee Harvey Oswald could have acted as a lone assassin.
Rex Features

From the moment of his father's death, John Kennedy Jnr *(right)* would become the focus of a million dreams that he might take on JFK's mantle and restore the idyll shattered by an assassin's bullets.
Hulton Deutsch Collection

known Valentino for many years and had been attending the crypt since the year he died. She kept coming until the 1960s. In the 1970s around 100 fans would mark the anniversary at the Hollywood Memorial Park, but by then ladies in black were rarely seen.

It seemed that, in the 1990s, only the jokers remained.

I decided to leave, but before I did I entered the white marble hallway of the Hollywood Cathedral Mausoleum, passed the ten-foot-high statues of saints, turned left into Corridor A and walked to the far end, where Crypt 1205 is. There, up against a stained-glass window with a scene of hillsides and cypresses that could be of Tuscany, was the tomb of Rodolpho Guglielmi Valentino. And it had flowers on it: a single pink chrysanthemum in each of two conical glass vases, one on either side of the nameplate. They were wilting, but could not have been there more than a day or so. I looked around, at all the hundreds of other crypts, and saw that none of them had flowers on them – none except Valentino's and the two beneath his. They were occupied by Virginia Ruth Mathis, and next to her, beneath Valentino, William D. Mathis. And I remembered that it was June Mathis, their daughter, who gave Valentino his big break.

I wondered again about the Lady in Black. On the way out I asked at the office, just to satisfy my curiosity. And to my surprise the woman behind the desk said, yes, there was a Lady in Black. She was called Estrellita de Reija and she came not once a year but every day to place flowers on Valentino's grave. Her mother's grave was here too, and she tended that as well. She marked for me on a green map of the cemetery where I would find it, just across a lake from Valentino.

'She claims that her mother was the original Lady in Black,' the woman said. 'And that her mother had an affair with Valentino and that she, Estrellita, is Valentino's daughter. I haven't seen her yet today, so you might catch her later. We all know her, she

97

talks to us. She comes in the office once a month to make a payment on a property here that she has for herself. She may talk to you, she may not, but she is . . . strange,' and she laughed.

I went with my map to find the place marked with a cross which was just past Cecil B. De Mille, to the east of John Huston and the west of Tyrone Power. From here, only the shallow lake separated the Lady in Black from Valentino.

Most of the graves were simple stones laid flush with the grass, with the occasional classically-styled family crypt and elaborate memorial dotted among the palms. Estrellita's mother's grave was like no other. Pink concrete edging bricks marked out an area some five by fifteen feet which was covered in large chips of white marble. In the centre of the area, which sloped right down to the lake shore, was a four-foot-tall white cement angel. A black headscarf had been placed on it, and the stems of two large red fabric roses slipped through the knot. At the lake end of the plot an old and rusted folding garden chair stood. On it were a green vase and a white vase, each containing clusters of pink and white fabric flowers. Gladioli had been scattered at the angel's feet.

I had to meet the Lady in Black.

I waited for a couple of hours but she did not come. I would return next day, but I couldn't make it until the afternoon, and I missed her. There were fresh white gladioli for Rudi.

The next day I waited for three hours but saw no sign of her, and the day after I missed her again. Rudi had white daisies today.

On the fifth day I was determined to meet Estrellita. I arrived shortly after eight, when the cemetery opened. There were no new flowers on Rudi's tomb. In the middle of the lake was an island, on which a temple stood. A footbridge led to it. I sat on the steps before the temple, from where I could look over the water, dotted with pink flowering water lilies, to the Lady in Black's grave. The water in the lake was very shallow and warm. Dozens of little fish flitted from my shadow.

All morning I waited, and was wondering whether I could hold out until closing time at 4.30, when I saw the unmistakable figure of Estrellita.

A little woman in black was walking swiftly along Lakeview Avenue, disappearing behind trees and bushes for periods, then reappearing by Cecil B. De Mille and coming down the slope to her mother. She carried a black shopping bag from which red gladioli protruded. I watched her as she gathered the dead flowers from the feet of the angel, bent them in two, and bundled them up in the paper she took from the new ones. Standing, she cradled the fresh flowers in her arm and scattered them one by one at the angel's feet. She picked around, tugging at weeds, adjusting the black headscarf on the white statue. I could vaguely hear her talking, but could not make out the words. Then she stood for a while, hands on hips, looking at the grave, before crossing herself, picking up her bag and moving off around the lake, headed for Valentino.

I went back over the footbridge and took the opposite route around the lake, walking slowly so that she would get to the mausoleum ahead of me. She turned the corner to Valentino's corridor as I entered. When I got to Rudi's section she was at the tomb. From her bag she took two bird of paradise flowers. 'Hello, Rudi,' she said, 'I'm here.'

Then she caught sight of me and looked annoyed. I quickly became very interested in the nameplates well away from Valentino's. She went back to her work, taking the dead flowers from Rudi's vases and replacing them with the bird of paradise blooms. She talked to herself as she did so, a low murmur, in Spanish.

'Beautiful flowers,' I said to her.

'Yes,' she said, 'very lovely. Perfect for him.'

Perhaps they were. They were certainly strikingly exotic, with their thick green stems, bright orange arrow-like leaves and flowers from which protruded slim purple tongues. Where the flower had sprung from the encasing stem there was a bright red lip to the edge of the wound.

'I came on the anniversary,' I said, 'but I didn't see you.'

She snorted. 'Look what they have done to Rudi's day. Were you here? And you wonder why I don't come on that day?'

I asked her how long she had been coming.

'Oh,' she grunted, 'a long time. And I will come every day for all of my life, for my mother and for Rudi.'

I asked her about her mother, and she said, 'You have many questions. Too many questions.'

I had plenty of questions, it was true. I wanted to ask her all about her mother's story, and her own, but abruptly she said goodbye and hurried off. I went with her to the entrance to the mausoleum, but she would say no more. At the door I stopped and watched her skirt the lake, cross herself once more beside her mother's grave, then disappear behind the trees, taking her secret with her.

CHAPTER SIX

The Road to Tara

SCARLETT O'HARA,
JONESBORO, GEORGIA, 31 AUGUST

At the Waffle House on Tara Boulevard, Jonesboro's official Scarlett O'Hara had dusted down the seat to her satisfaction and was ordering breakfast.

'I'll have the scrambled cheese eggs,' she said. 'And raisin toast. But I want no butter on my toast. And no extra butter on my grits. And bacon. And decaf coffee.'

And after each new little order I half expected the waitress to murmur, 'No Miss Scarlett. Yes Miss Scarlett. Miss Scarlett, I'm glad to see you's eating cos if you ent you ent going to no barbecue at Twelve Oaks.'

Why fiddle de dee.

I had come to Jonesboro, a half-hour's drive south of Atlanta, Georgia, in search of the fans of *Gone With the Wind* – who happily style themselves Windies – of Scarlett O'Hara, and of Tara, her home. Would I find the relics? Did the Windies? Up to a point, everyone had told me. But don't hope for the earth.

This trip was different from the other journeys I was making around America. By looking at a character who was pure fiction I knew I could not learn anything from it about the nature of stardom. But Scarlett O'Hara was undoubtedly a heroine, and a very powerful figure – despite the fact that she had never existed. And what fascinated me was the way in which so many women wanted to become her in any small way

101

that they could – by playing her in a TV movie, by exploiting some physical resemblance to her, by collecting relics associated with *Gone With the Wind*. There were even, I was to discover, women who had grown up believing that they *were* Scarlett.

Certainly, if you are looking for Tara and Scarlett, Jonesboro is the place to come. Now a little dormitory town half swallowed into metropolitan Atlanta, it styles itself The Home of *Gone With the Wind*. This is no idle boast. In Margaret Mitchell's book and David O. Selznick's film, Jonesboro is a microcosm of the South, and of the havoc wrought by the Civil War. We see it go from prosperous county seat, surrounded by the fine homes of rich plantation-owners, to devastation during Sherman's campaign to sack Atlanta, and to a burned-out shell overwhelmed by carpet-baggers and rogues. Mitchell's is a meticulously accurate picture of Jonesboro both geographically and historically, the canvas on which the powerful figure of Scarlett O'Hara struggles against almost insuperable odds to hang onto the red earth of Tara, her home.

But Jonesboro today is by no means immediately recognizable from the film or the novel. The Jonesboro road south from Atlanta, on which Scarlett fled the burning city, heading back to Tara in a broken-down carriage pulled by a broken-down horse, is now a four-lane highway through sub-suburban Atlanta. Only the names give a clue to the connection. In Jonesboro, the Old Dixie Highway – Route 3 – is named Tara Boulevard. On this street and others in the town you will spot Tara Auto Sales, Tara Pawn, Tara Methodist Church, Tara State Bank, Tara Beach, O'Hara's liquor store, a housing estate named after Twelve Oaks and another called Ashley Woods, both offered for sale through Tara Realty.

At Hooters, a bar on Tara Boulevard, where rednecks drink jugs of beer, gnaw their way through buckets of fried seafood and ogle the waitresses in their uniforms of cut-off T-shirt and orange hot pants, the menu makes leering reference to Scarlett, 'beautiful local lady' and invites: 'Take a look at our southern belles'. Yee-haw!

When I arrived, the afternoon before my breakfast with Scarlett, I drove into Jonesboro's tiny, half-abandoned downtown, following the railroad tracks behind a car that sported the bumper sticker 'Thank you Charles J. Giles for wealth without risk', past a store called 'Dance with Donna Webb. The Southern Motion Cloggers' and pulled up beside the railroad depot. This was the station which, on the last day of August and the first day of September 1864, northern troops burned to cut off Atlanta's last link with the south, where they ripped up three miles of railroad tracks, heaping the rails on bonfires and then twisting them around telegraph poles.

On the hill to the east stands the court-house in which Margaret Mitchell did much of her research for *Gone With the Wind*, fleshing out childhood memories of summers spent on the Fitzgerald Plantation, her grandparents' farm in Jonesboro. Its clocktower looks out now from behind sixties two-storey extensions on all sides. The railway depot, rebuilt in 1867, houses a shop called Tara Relics. You can buy a snub-nosed lead confederate bullet for $1, or one whittled by a soldier in the dull periods between murderous activity for $2. There are spent bullets too, deformed by impact. And there are letters from soldiers on sale, frightened missives to loved ones. They read like fresh blood from an old wound. Such mementoes sit ill with the garish Scarlett dolls, the *Gone With the Wind* plates, not to mention the Elvis posters.

Around the corner is an ante-bellum (pre Civil War) mansion called Stately Oaks, transported here by the local historical society and surrounded by a high mesh fence to keep out the stone-throwing vandals who are less interested in preserving their heritage than smashing it up.

Gone With the Wind has a strange, compelling power. It is arguably the most popular novel of all time. It sold a million copies in the first six months of publication in 1936 — at the height of the Depression — and 28 million to date, in 155 editions in twenty-seven languages. It has sold more copies than any book in history except the Bible.

When it was announced that the novel would be filmed, the whole of America had a view on who should play Scarlett. The search took two years and cost over $92,000. 1,400 actresses were seen and ninety screen-tested. When a Selznick employee visited Atlanta in search of Scarlett there were mob scenes. Countless women were convinced that not only were they born to play Scarlett, they *were* Scarlett. Fans wrote to Selznick and Margaret Mitchell begging that their favourite actress get the part, arguing that it was impossible for anyone but Kate Hepburn, Joan Crawford or whoever to play her. Bette Davis turned it down twice. Finally, when the part went to Vivien Leigh, a foreigner, there was uproar. Protests poured in to Selznick. 'Why not cast Chiang Kai-shek?' raged one fan.

The film lifted the characters of Scarlett and Rhett to the pinnacle of American popular culture. They were seen as ideals of man and womanhood. Millions aspired to be like them, and in Atlanta, anyone who resembles them can still become a star.

When plans were announced to turn the sequel, *Scarlett*, written by Alexandra Ripley, into a TV mini series, 20,000 women auditioned for the part of Scarlett. Such was the power of the myth surrounding the original search for Scarlett that the producers of the sequel mirrored it, right down to eventually choosing an Englishwoman, Joanne Whalley-Kilmer. Melly Meadows, Jonesboro's official Scarlett O'Hara, got to the last twenty-three, one of only five women from the USA and the only one from the South to stand the course.

Melly was telling me, as she shovelled down her Waffle House eggs with the gusto of a true Scarlett, how she entered her first lookalike contest in 1986, at the age of sixteen, and won, and describing all the amazing coincidences about the whole thing. It's pretty unusual to look just like Scarlett as portrayed by Vivien Leigh. But to look like her and to be from the very same little town (pop. 4,132) that Scarlett was from . . . and to be named Melly, short for Melanie, the very name of Scarlett's rival for the wimpish Ashley Wilkes . . . amazing.

I could tell the diners around us thought it was amazing too. Activity had slowed in the restaurant as Melly held forth, playing to the room rather than merely talking to me. Conversations were hushed, the better to take in the story of one young woman who seemed to be living that potent dream of being Scarlett.

It was strange having breakfast with someone who is a dead ringer for Vivien Leigh. Melly is striking. Her eyes are almost luminous, a bright hazel with flecks of grey at the edges. Her wavy dark hair is pulled back from her forehead. The lower half of her face is slightly squarer, her lips a little fuller than Vivien's. She has a little turned-up section beneath her nose, and two big square white front teeth.

When I had got over the initial shock of Melly's physical resemblance to Scarlett I began to look for signs of similarity in her character. Scarlett in book and film is a wild young thing, schooled in daintiness, dressed in finery, but with an untamed soul that showed itself through those green, green eyes. Turbulent, wilful, lusty with life is how Margaret Mitchell describes her on the opening page of *Gone With the Wind*. Was Melly's Scarlett any more than skin deep?

Finishing her eggs, she daintily picked up a crisp sliver of bacon between thumb and forefinger and nibbled at it as she told me about the first time she saw the film properly. 'It was on TV,' she said, 'and at the end of the movie when Rhett left Scarlett, honest to goodness for twenty minutes I had a breakdown. I sobbed and I cried and my sister, who is eleven months older, she just sat and she stroked my hair and she rocked me and she said, "Melly it's OK. It's just a story, it didn't really happen." I was shaking, I was so upset and I said, "I have to know if they get back together. I can't stand it. That's too beautiful, she was so wrong and he was so right."'

The waitress, who had come by to top up our coffee cups during this tale, was caught up in the recollected emotion and stood at the table until it was over, um-humming in sympathy.

Being Scarlett was something any Southern girl would like to do, said Melly, moving on to her raisin toast, which she spread with apple jelly. She was SOOOOO lucky to have this opportunity. She has toured Japan as Scarlett, been to France, she has welcomed to Atlanta the International Olympic Committee delegates, Japanese prime minister Kaifu, the 1988 Democratic Convention. She is official Scarlett O'Hara spokesperson for MGM/UA Home Video. Four or five times a week she is Scarlett for a fee, and fifty times she has gone into local schools on a Scarlett-says-no-to-drugs campaign.

Dressing as Scarlett was just the divinest thing, she went on. 'The dresses, the lace and the ruffles and bows on your pantaloons make any woman feel the most feminine she could feel. The men treat you differently. They become chivalrous. I find everyday average men in blue jeans stopping and bowing to me on the street. "Morning Miss Scarlett." Tipping baseball caps to me. When you wear a beautiful dress like that (I have nine modelled on Scarlett's clothes from the movie), people treat you like a lady and you feel like a lady and feminine and beautiful. It doesn't matter how your face looks, you are still beautiful when you have on a dress like that.'

But what, I asked her, was Scarlett's appeal? Wasn't she just a spoiled, coquettish brat whose so-called charm was of such a saccharine consistency that it gave you toothache?

106

'Excuse me?' said Melly as if I had just uttered a blasphemy, and then leaped to the defence of her heroine.

'Scarlett is the kind of woman EVERY man loves,' she said a little pointedly, 'and every woman envies. She is beautiful but not in a real earthly way. She has a beauty about her which is not just the way her face looks. She dares to be different. In a world that was only for men she was a businesswoman, she knew what she wanted and she got it. In the sequel she gets Rhett. She has enough guts that she doesn't care what other people think, and there are a lot of women who wish they were that way but don't have the courage.'

She paused, as if sensing she was on the winning straight, before finishing me off with: 'There are a lot of men who would love to love a woman like that but don't have the courage to go after her.'

I wondered if Melly-as-Scarlett attracted the attention of modern-day Rhetts. 'No, not at all. Because I don't present myself that way. I present the Scarlett who has charms, like the child who makes you a Valentine's card, you are charmed by it, it is sincere.'

In any case, she confided once she thought my tape recorder was switched off, Rhetts are hard to find. One she took to a party got drunk and disgraced himself. She was so embarrassed! She never, ever used him again!

In Melly's opinion, the closest Atlanta has to a Rhett today is Ted Turner, owner of CNN and, through his purchase of the Metro-Goldwyn-Mayer film library, of *Gone With the Wind* itself. If you buy the video the first name you see on the screen is Turner. He is a *Gone With the Wind* obsessive too. He has a son named Rhett, Melly told me, and I had read of how, when the film was premiered in Russia a few years ago, Turner went with it and made a speech in which he told the Russian people that they, like the American South, like his people, like Scarlett, could rebuild and prevail.

When Ted wants a Scarlett he calls Melly.

'I met Ted at a video convention in Vegas,' she said, 'when I was appearing as Scarlett. I went up to him and I said, "You handsome thing you, you have to be Captain Rhett Butler himself."

'Very modestly he pulled out his convention name-badge from his pocket and he said, "Oh no, really, I'm just Ted Turner," and showed me his name.'

Melly told me all the thousands of tourists who came to Atlanta, to Jonesboro, looking for the real Tara would be disappointed. The Japanese were the hardest to convince. Since Japan Airlines began their daily flights to Atlanta from Tokyo the Japanese had been pouring in, fascinated by *Gone With the Wind* – perhaps because the story parallels their experience of rebuilding a shattered economy and civilization after defeat in a war – convinced that if they just looked hard enough they would find Tara.

'Tara is not a real place. *Gone With the Wind* is not a land you can visit,' she said, looking me straight in the eye, 'it's a place in your heart.'

I thanked her for sharing that with me.

I found plenty of people obsessed with *Gone With the Wind* in Jonesboro. I met three Scarlett O'Haras in a week. One of them I came across by accident, misdialling Melly's number and getting a girl who said wait a minute, I do Scarlett too. I could have met more, but realized that I would not find what I was looking for. These girls had not caught the true obsession. They weren't like Scarlett, they hadn't really thought about what she was, they weren't captivated by her power, they just liked the frocks: dressing-up for grown-ups.

I gave up on these self-proclaimed Scarletts and headed into Atlanta proper for an afternoon on the trail of Margaret Mitchell herself.

Margaret Mitchell was just four feet eleven inches tall, slim and lithe, with striking looks rather than beauty. Her first marriage, to a sub-standard Rhett Butler type called Berrien Kinnard, lasted just a few months. She divorced him in favour of a mild-mannered Ashley Wilkes of a man, John Marsh.

The pickings in Atlanta were slim, the city uninspiring. Within its encircling freeway I found a city of low-rise and empty lots, loosely scattered over low hills with, at its heart, its modest cluster of high-rise. There was the round silver and black one that resembled a giant gas canister, the charcoal grey one topped with what looked like littered building blocks, as if constructed by a child who got bored with the game, the ochre pyramid, the twin art deco towers. I found Peachtree, the street that is Atlanta's main thoroughfare and which gets plenty of mentions in *Gone With the Wind*, and followed it north, looking for Mitchell's house. This is the street that swarms with life in the novel, packed with the soldiers of the South when it is still the powerhouse of the Confederacy, that blazes when Atlanta falls. North of downtown, at the junction of West Peachtree Street and Tenth Street, I found the house Mitchell lived in when she wrote much of the novel.

The Dump is a three-storey, brick Tudor-revival house that must once have been very grand. Today its roof is swathed in plastic sheeting. Yellow ropes holding the plastic in place come down the walls and are tied to stakes driven into the ground. It wasn't much to look at when Margaret Mitchell and John Marsh moved here in 1925 to rent a poky basement apartment at the back, its once handsome front defaced with a complex run of iron fire escapes zigzagging all over it. Today it is barely standing. On one of its boarded windows someone has scrawled in brown paint the plea: Save Me! A TV aerial which had lost its footing on the roof hung on the end of its wire a few feet above the ground, swinging in the warm breeze. Around the other side a corner of the building had fallen away, bringing a three-storey stack of bathrooms crashing down, leaving just the taps and sinks on the walls and the toilet-roll holders behind the modestly closed doors.

Yes, the house was well named: it was a dump.

Mitchell sites were few and far between in Atlanta. They had some of her belongings in the public library, and if I had been here a few weeks later I might have gone to the Georgian Terrace, where the stars stayed for the 1939 première of the movie, and where a museum called The Road to Tara was to open. There is also the Oakland cemetery, where Mitchell is buried in the family plot. The cemetery is out through the public housing projects along a street named after another famous Atlantean, Martin Luther King.

I did drive three blocks north of the Dump, to the spot where Mitchell died in 1949. She was crossing Peachtree at 13th with her husband. They were on their way to the cinema to see *The Canterbury Tales* when a taxi ran her down. Not much of a way to go. No heroic struggle there, just a splat. There is a Texaco on one corner now, tower blocks on the other three, but no plaque to Margaret Mitchell.

A derelict house, an anonymous crossroads – it wasn't much to hold onto. I could see why the Windies left disappointed.

I did meet a Rhett Butler lookalike, who was obsessed enough to be fun.

Davis Spohn even has his own American Express credit card in the name of Captain Rhett Butler. He uses it when he is on a trip and will be appearing as Rhett. He's a bit of a method actor, is David.

The card is a real one, given to him by American Express after he appeared in an ad with them as Rhett and, referring to Butler's home town in South Carolina, delivered the punch line: 'I wouldn't leave Charleston without it.'

Now, if in stores or hotels they think the card must be a fake, David invites them to call up AmEx, who say, 'Yes sir, Captain Butler has very good credit with us.'

Spohn gives the strong impression that he would rather be Rhett Butler, great romantic creation, or Clark Gable, dashing movie star, ladies' man and man's man, than David Spohn, who travels America teaching insurance brokers how to sell insurance. And when he isn't pretending to be either of them, which he had done 490 times when I met him, when he isn't watching *Gone With the Wind*, which he has done fifty-four times – not counting the times he has listened to the soundtrack on tape in his car, driving to a booking – he is compiling lists of the things he and Gable have in common.

There are 126 of them. 'Down to our blood type. We both like turtle-neck shirts. Our favourite meal is rare steak and a baked potato. Our second favourite meal is chicken with dumplings. Clark ate English-style with the fork turned down, which I have learned to do. Clark could not wear a ring on his index finger because it was broken when he was working on the oilfields with his dad. I have a scar here where I did some arc welding so I can't wear a ring here either, so we both wear pinkie rings. We both like tiger eyes and onyx.

'We both like to ride, both collect weapons, both love to shoot and hunt, both had large dogs. He had a red Labrador retriever named Bobby, I had a Dobermann. I also had a German Shepherd. We both love animals, like kids and have owned horses.

'I like to work on cars and so did he. He boxed, I took karate. We were born on a Friday. I was premature otherwise I'd have been born the first week of February; he was born the first week in February. We both volunteered during a war, he in World War Two, me in Vietnam, Desert Shield and Desert Storm. We both were in our forties, twice the age of the guys that we were fighting with. We were not pilots but we both flew in combat. He was an aerial gunner, I was a medic. We both got along great with our people and a lot of people looked up to us.

'Clark was the only guy with false teeth that had got canines. When I met the dentist from Gable's bomb squadron he wanted to look in my mouth. I had canines and the dentist said, "I don't believe it, this is getting scary."'

Are we at 126 yet? Quite honestly my eyes had glazed over and I had stopped counting, so I was glad when David changed the subject and told me how, often, he will slip into the part of Rhett or Clark without realizing it. He discovered he could do so quite by chance in a lookalike contest which he entered, and won, in 1985. The judges asked him what he would do to win the affections of Scarlett O'Hara. Without thinking he said: 'Well frankly old boy I'd give her anything that her little black heart desires, and a few things that she doesn't.'

'I have fans. I get mail,' he continued. 'A lot of mail. Little Valentine's Day cards. They write to Rhett, I get stuff all the time.'

Any panties? Nude photographs? Demands to bear his child? He gave me a look that suggested I ought to start being a gentleman right there and then, but I gave one last probe. Didn't people think he was taking things a bit far, I asked, when he applied to join the Atlanta public library – as he has done – or the Smithsonian Institute, under the name Rhett Butler?

'I haven't had any complaints so far,' he said, unperturbed, adding that he also had the Post Office box PO 1864, Jonesboro. 'The year and the place of *Gone With the Wind*. Took me two years to get it.'

There were *Gone With the Wind* collectors to meet, too. One called Ron Hudgins had the cheque for $300 back taxes, which is shown in a close-up in the movie, and a brick from the porch of Tara, one of the bricks Vivien Leigh sits on at the start of the movie when she is flirting with the Tarleton twins. And in the front garden of his suburban chalet bungalow he has the gravestone of a Confederate soldier. No-one he knows.

Another man, called Herb Bridges, has, in a collection that is probably the finest in the world, the Paris bonnet which Rhett Butler brings to Scarlett during the wartime blockade of Atlanta and which she puts on upside down, she being so out of touch with Paris fashion. He also has the mourning hat that she wears. He dug it out for me to see, though he claimed he couldn't find the Paris bonnet.

'It's very crudely made,' he said apologetically. 'It wasn't meant to last. You didn't get that close up to it.' We struggled to arrange its couple of yards of net. 'Let me see,' said Herb, 'it's an awful lot of veil. That goes down all around her arms. I think this kind of crinkly bit went over the top something like that.'

Herb's house was twenty miles south-west of Jonesboro, out towards another little town called Newnan, which had all the charm that Jonesboro lacked. Built around a court-house square it was a hospital town – for both sides – during the Civil War. It is a few miles from the Chattahoochee River which formed a barrier which for a time held back the northern troops. I enjoyed the drive to it through the pine forest and the gently undulating countryside. On the way I stopped for a while where the road crossed the flint-grey Flint River, on the banks of which the fictional Tara stood. The muddy waters swirled around an abandoned washing machine and the traffic galumped over the concrete planks of the bridge beside me, heavy-metal music blasting from the open window of a pick-up truck. Not a romantic spot.

I mentioned this place to Herb and he, like Melly, shook his head and said that if you want to see Tara we have nothing at all to show you.

But he could show me a bit of the old South, at a restaurant called Sprayberry's Pit Barbecue (motto: Pig out at Sprayberry's) where, in a pit outside, pork and beef joints cook over hickory charcoal for eight hours. I got a barbecue plate which included a bowl of Brunswick stew, like a thick soup of meat fragments, and a mound of barbecued meat stirred into a sauce of a sweet and sourness that approximates remarkably closely to stomach juices. I hadn't tasted anything like it since I last threw up. I half expected to see my dinner digesting right there on my plate.

'Now this,' Herb said proudly, indicating the food, 'is exactly what would have been eaten at the Twelve Oaks barbecue. This restaurant is nationally famous. Dan Quayle has eaten here.'

That clinched it for me.

Newnan was pleasant, and I hung around for a couple of days, meeting the airline pilots and rich doctors who had bought many of its wonderful antebellum mansions and were spending millions refurbishing them.

One of them told me about a local woman called Carolyn Busby. You should meet her, I was told, she has a window and a shutter from Tara. I was a little doubtful, having met so many collectors and impersonators already, but I phoned her, and I'm glad I did.

Because she turned out to be Scarlett. And she led me to the real Tara.

Sure I could see her relics from Tara, she said. She lived six miles away down a snaking road that wove through steaming hot pine woods to her Greek revival house in the little hamlet of Roscoe. This is an eerily backward place where you can still see Civil War trenches down near the river, if you can brave the waist-deep mud and the snakes, and where the graveyard in the local church is home to Confederate soldiers, Yankees and slaves.

Going to Carolyn's house was like travelling back in time, to a past that she still lives in. Her house was a beautifully preserved single-storey, four-room Louisiana-style plantation house, she told me. It had a wide hall that would be opened at both ends to allow the breeze to flow through. Before her divorce she had run an antiques business, which explained the period furniture, but when her marriage broke up she bought this place, then a wreck on a plot in Newnan, and had it transported out to Roscoe, setting it down in a clearing cut from the steamy woods.

'We've had a terrible time with mildew,' she said. 'These frame houses are just black, you can't keep it off. It's the humidity. In winter it just rains all the time and it dun't quit.'

She showed me around.

'That's my great-grandfather in the Civil War uniform,' she said, pointing to a print made from a daguerreotype. 'He was named George Horton and he came through the war. He was very handsome and I'm very proud to have his picture. I have letters written home by him. The sense of family history is very common in the South. That's the big difference between us and the North. We are so caught up in our backgrounds, at least from my generation. The Civil War is very vivid. I heard all the stories from my mother. I heard about my ancestor being taken out of her home and put on a mattress in front while they burned the house down. That's my kinfolks they did this to. I've heard it all, right from a child, and it's ingrained.'

Between my telephoning Carolyn and arriving at her house she had spoken to her lawyer, who advised against letting me see the window, for security reasons. Only the shutter, a dusty green, was leaning against the wall in her hall beside a photo of Mammie, Scarlett's black maid, peering through a window – her window? She apologized for her caution, but said that within weeks the window would be on show in the new Atlanta museum called The Road to Tara along with Ronald's gear. But not Herb's. Herb couldn't agree terms.

Gone With the Wind fans were overwhelmed when they saw her window and shutter, she said. 'The Japanese in particular just go crazy. They want to have their picture taken with it. The president of the Coca-Cola bottling company in Japan came here with his wife, he would touch it, he would stand back from it and say, "Can you believe this? The window from Tara!" They just love it, it's like a shrine. I have a lot of fun with it. But it's so valuable now that I'll feel more comfortable when it's in the museum.'

We came to her bedroom. I admired the bed. 'That's my Scarlett bed,' she said, and laughed a little self-consciously.

I asked her if she identified with Scarlett and she looked down at her hands, saying, 'Well, you're going to think this sounds more than a little silly, I am sure, but I was Scarlett. I grew up knowing I was her. Oh, I know she is in every Southern woman, but with me it was much more than that. Right from the age of thirteen I was raised as Scarlett. I am Scarlett.'

So Scarlett wasn't an actress in her mid-twenties, she was this slight, fair-haired, bespectacled, rather staid and bookish woman with the sensible shoes.

This would take some getting used to.

Carolyn was embarrassed at having told me, and tried to back off from the subject, but when she realized that I wasn't laughing she led me through to her dining-room, its walls made from plain, hewn pine planks, darkened with the years, to show me her most valued possession, a faded and cracked scrap-album which contained the mementoes of her finest hour.

In 1961, she told me, they had a Civil War centennial ball in Atlanta. It was the biggest thing that ever hit the city. Vivien Leigh came and Olivia de Havilland, who played Melly in the film, and all the Southern governors.

'This is my *Gone With the Wind* scrap-book. Here is a drawing I did of the dress I wore to the ball. That's me in my dress.'

'You do look like Scarlett,' I said.

'Well, I remember that as I walked in, there was a man. He was a little bit intoxicated. He was sitting in the lobby and when I arrived he stood up and said, "My God there is Scarlett," and it just made my whole night. But I did look like her. My date dressed like Ashley. I

116

like Rhett better now that I have got older. Right then, at sixteen, I preferred Ashley.'

'Who was your date?' I asked her.

'I can't even remember his name. No, wait, he was called Al Miller. I met him one night of my life, it was kind of a blind date. That's all, I don't remember anything else about him.

'I made the papers. Here are my pantaloons. I did the whole thing. Here is my Vivien Leigh autograph. For two weeks beforehand you couldn't read about anything else in the paper, you couldn't get tickets. This was more than an inauguration in Washington. This was the biggest thing.

'Oh I cannot tell you! It was the best night of my life. I don't even remember the food and drink, I just remember the confederate flags around the ceiling, and I still have my souvenir from the ball. I remember the band played Dixie every other song.

'Al Miller I didn't like at all. When I think back we left before the thing was over. I get angry now when I think of it. I was so young at the time. I just let him steer me around and he says it's time to go and well, you know, I have to go. Now I wouldn't do that. Now I'd say, "You go, I'm staying."

'The most exciting night of my life . . .' she mused over the statement, smiling to herself. 'I said that to somebody once and they said well you must have had a pretty dull life. But I really haven't. Yet it was the most exciting, more than my wedding. History became real, it was marvellous, I got to look like Scarlett. I was Scarlett.'

As she closed the book I asked her how she got her window and shutter, and what happened to the rest of Tara. She told me the Tara film set left California in 1959. It was bought by two Atlanta businessmen, Julian Foster, a developer, and Robert Troutman, a lawyer. There was a big ceremony when Tara came back to Atlanta, a celebration on the Capitol steps. The band played Dixie, the governor was there, and

Miss Atlanta. Foster and Troutman planned to recreate Tara in Atlanta, but it never came off. Instead, the building was stored in a barn.

A friend of Carolyn's, Betty Talmadge, the wife of a Georgia senator, made an offer in the 1970s. 'They wanted $200,000, she knocked them down to $5,000,' said Carolyn. 'Betty is a real horse-trader. He told her a window and a shutter were missing. I used to lie awake at night wondering where they were. Then they cropped up, they were in a little museum for a few years, I read about them in a newspaper. In the end I was able to buy them.

'On the morning Betty was to do the deal for the rest of Tara, Foster didn't show up. He had died. The deal was finally signed by his widow, but she had no idea where the thing was stored, except that it was in a barn to the north of the city somewhere. Betty did everything to find it, hired an ex-cop to search the area calling at all the farms, chartered a light plane to fly over and see if there were barns he might not have found. Finally when they were going through Foster's things they found cancelled cheques to a farmer, and Tara was discovered. For ten years she tried to put it up somewhere. Clayton county, which Jonesboro is part of, and Calloway county, which is where Newnan is, were both interested but it came to nothing. In the end she gave her stuff to the Atlanta Historical Society who have it in storage.'

But maybe I would like to visit Betty's home anyway, because the Lovejoy Plantation had been well-known to Margaret Mitchell and was the model for Twelve Oaks. More importantly, the model for Tara in the book, the Fitzgerald Plantation house, home of Margaret Mitchell's grandparents, had also been moved there from its original site four miles away when it was threatened with demolition.

So, never mind any movie set. The real Tara *did* exist. And this was the first I had heard of it, in a week of talking to *Gone With the Wind* fanatics.

I drove over that afternoon, through a fine summer rain. I asked Carolyn to come with me, tickled by the idea of driving up to Tara and Twelve Oaks with Scarlett, but she said no, she had shopping to do. So I was alone as I approached the house up a long private drive through pine woods. The fields opened out before me. There was the model for Twelve Oaks to the left, and to the right, across a field and behind two towering oaks, an old ruined house.

I knocked at the back door of the Lovejoy Plantation. Through the mesh screen I could see a TV flickering. My knock was answered by a woman who told me her name was Dee. She held the door open just a crack against the rain. Mrs Talmadge was not here, she told me. She had undergone surgery the day before and was still in hospital. I could look around if I wanted to. And she shut the door on me as she went to get a leaflet. It seemed they did tours – but only for groups and only if booked in advance. She came back and thrust the leaflet out at me, saying she was sorry but she had a call holding. That's Tara over there, she said, pointing to the wreck in the field. 'They took the Victorian front off and the settler's cabin part.'

I opened the leaflet, which was quickly spotted with rain. 'Come to the scenic Old South,' I read. 'It still exists. Among the tall pines and ancient live oaks of Tara Country, Lovejoy Plantation – inspiration for Ashley Wilkes's Twelve Oaks in *Gone With the Wind* – sits in Southern Splendor, gracious remnant of a glorious past.'

I walked around to the front of the house, deciding to save Tara itself to last. The house was impressive, with six fluted Doric columns supporting a broad, two-storey porch with a long hanging balcony on the second floor. Cocooned in its 1,200 acres, Lovejoy was a peaceful, time-locked place, immune to the modern world just as Roscoe, and Carolyn Busby, seemed to be.

There were stories about the house, my soggy leaflet told me. One that the columns were hollow, and had been filled with grain after the fall of Atlanta, to keep it from the Yankees. Another, which forms a part of *Gone With the Wind*, is that a woman of the house fired down from the stairs on a Yankee deserter who had come to loot the property. I walked around to the side, where a swimming-pool was dotted with black leaves. Before a paddock in which a chestnut mare stood, head bowed in the rain, there was a little rustic outbuilding filled with mementoes. There was a still that I remembered seeing in *Gone With the Wind* and, written in the cement when wet, the information: 'Tara movie set 1939 GWTW.'

I retraced my steps to the other side of the house where the farm buildings were. There was a long, open-sided barn empty but for a pick-up. Before the barn and a large black mesh satellite dish was a notice-board headed Lovejoy Plantation Personnel.

It was a jokey thing, giving farm animals names culled from *Gone With the Wind* and from principals in the Civil War:

Billy T. Sherman
Clark Gobble
Abaaham Lincoln
Assley Wilkes
Ulysses S. Grunt
Rabbit E. Lee
Belle Wadlin
Uncle Prettypat
Scarlett O'Hen
Sen John C. Cowhoun

Some of the animals had houses on the grass beside the drive. One was marked 'Lovejoy Fire House, home of Billy T. Sherman', another 'Home of Rabbit E. Lee'.

The rain grew heavy as I walked across to the field and Tara, or the Fitzgerald place. It was in a sorry state, jacked up on cinder blocks, the roof covered in black plastic sheeting lifted at one corner by the wind, folded back to reveal decaying green felt. It was just the shell of the main house, denuded of its porch and verandahs, with two doors and four windows, the wood blackened. Beside it stood a single-storey section, the original settler's home that Dee had mentioned. It was in an even worse state: the cinder-block supports had fallen away under the right-hand side of the building and it slumped, deflated, to the ground. This was the rambling house of the novel, but it had nothing to do with the pillared and porticoed Tara that was invented for the movie in Hollywood.

Philip Fitzgerald, Margaret Mitchell's great-grandfather, had come from County Tipperary in 1831 and been a pioneer settler in the area, building up a holding before the war of 2,375 acres and owning thirty-five slaves. In this house he and his wife Eleanor had raised seven daughters. One of them – Annie – married an Atlantean called John Stephens, and they were Margaret Mitchell's grandparents. Margaret, as a child, came to stay with Annie and John in this house.

For all those Windies who came in search of the real thing and were told it did not exist, here was the proof that it did, though the reality might not measure up to the movie fiction. It seemed good enough to me though, and I walked the dirt track which skirted the field for a closer look. As I did so the rain came pouring down, forming little lakes on the grass, making the sorry house look sorrier still.

I looked down and noticed that, on the dirt track at my feet, the rain was forming orange puddles on the red earth of Tara.

CHAPTER SEVEN

The Death Drive

JAMES DEAN,
CHOLAME, CALIFORNIA, 30 SEPTEMBER

This was it. This was really it. At the very same moment, in the very same place.

Man, they muttered to each other, it was so real you could taste it.

At exactly this time, 5.45 p.m. on 30 September 1955, James Dean's silver Porsche Spyder had breasted the hot cashmere hills to the east, dropped swiftly down the narrow, straight road through the desert, closing fast on the intersection at which they now stood.

In those same seconds the sun was setting behind the hills to the west, sending out that very same, blinding, eye-level flash before it dipped out of sight. They turned to the west, to get that momentary burn on the back of their eyeballs, and knew that their eyes felt exactly as Jimmy Dean's had, knew they were seeing things exactly as he had seen them.

But they knew something that Jimmy did not. They knew that death was speeding towards him from within that white light.

As they turned to face east once more, as someone solemnly counted down the final fifteen seconds in the life of the very first teenager, they knew they stood in the same eerie shadowless glow, suspended between day and night, the glow that Jimmy Dean had disappeared into.

They were so into the mood of it that as the count-down passed 5 and 4 and 3 they could almost see that great, lumbering 1950 black and white Ford come up to the Y-junction from the west, see the driver swing the wheel to turn left across Jimmy's path, hear the first skid as he fatally hesitated, unable to decide whether he could beat the Porsche to the junction. They could almost see Jimmy's tiny, low-slung aluminium sports car flash through those final few yards, hear the second squeal of the Ford's rubber as the driver, having taken his foot off the brake once to go for the gap, decided finally that it was impossible.

And then they really could see the Porsche. And it was at the intersection. But there was no black and white Ford. And as they watched, as the countdown went from one to zero, Jimmy's car went safely over the junction, passing right through death and out the other side. And as he drew level with the little throng of James Dean fanatics, lookalikes, conspiracy theorists and vintage-car buffs, the driver sounded his horn and raised two fingers in a victory sign. And after a startled moment's silence they let out a chorus of cheers, whoops and whistles that followed the Porsche as it sped on into the east, to complete Jimmy's journey to Paso Robles in safety.

James Dean lived. It was a miracle.

Alternatively it was a load of rubbish, witnessed by a bunch of sad people who had spent nearly forty years wishing that they could rewrite history. James Dean fanatics were the most extreme fans I had come across, but I could not pretend that I was totally immune to the appeal of this little ceremony. And I was certainly not immune to the appeal of James Dean. So when I heard about the Death Drive, I was itching to go along on it. The idea of retracing his final journey was appealing and repellent at the same time. It was a sick idea and yet irresistible, like rubbernecking at the scene of a car crash. Everyone condemns those who do it. And everyone does it.

For the most dedicated, the day had begun at 8 a.m., a day in which every second counted and therefore should be relived and remembered. It had begun at 1219 North Vine, which used to be Competition Motors, where Jimmy had bought his Porsche and where he and Rolf Wutherich, his mechanic, had some final checks made on the car. They were headed 300 miles north, to Salinas, where Jimmy was to take part in a race the next day. Tonight they would stop over in Paso Robles, 150 miles away.

No detail from that day was too small, too insignificant. At noon Jimmy had lunch with his father Winton Dean and grandfather Charlie Dean at the Farmer's Market on 3rd and Fairfax. Jimmy ate a sandwich and drank a glass of milk. So the Death Drivers had the same.

At 1.30 Jimmy and Rolf went to pick up the other two members of their party, the photographer Sandy Roth and Bill Hickman. With Jimmy and Rolf in the Spyder and the others following in his station wagon, the journey began.

And the Death Drivers had studied the route, memorized the stops, knew where the new roads differed from Jimmy's 1955 route, where you could sneak off onto the old roads and where you could not. They knew that the Hollywood Freeway which he took out of town ended, in '55, at Lankersham, so you should get off there, make a left, then a right on Ventura and follow Ventura all the way out to Sepulveda.

They knew where he stopped for gas on Ventura Boulevard. It was not a gas station now. It sold flowers. But there it was still, right by Casa de Cadillac, the pumps gone but the islands still in place. You could get out and stand right where Jimmy stood. All the Dean picture books had the shot Roth took that day of Jimmy by the Porsche, the station wagon in the background.

The picture showed that he had stripped off his turtle-neck by now. Jimmy was down to a white T-shirt, the white T-shirt on which his blood was spilled. It had been a hot day in '55, way up in the 90s. It was as hot today as it had been then, which was good. It brought the Death Drivers closer to feeling just how Jimmy felt.

Sepulveda Boulevard took them to the Golden State Freeway, but in '55 there was no freeway and those who knew how took the old road right out past Valencia.

Here Jimmy stopped at Tip's Diner for a glass of milk, but the fans would ignore the faded red and white Tip's sign sailing high above the treetops and loop round under the freeway to a Wendy's. Because, as they would tell anyone who needed to know, Tip's had changed its location. In '55 it was here.

And if you thought, no big deal, who wants to go to a Wendy's, you just didn't understand what this was all about. Because it was here that you came upon the first great big 'if only . . .' And you needed to stop and think about it for a few minutes, weigh the gravity of the insignificant little happening here against the fact that anything, any little thing, that would have deflected Jimmy from that fatal time-scale, that tragic countdown to death, would have meant that he was saved.

And what happened here was that two young waitresses, Estelle and her buddy – history had forgotten the name of the second girl – recognized Jimmy and were urging each other to go up to him and get his autograph. But they were too shy. Finally, just as the Porsche was backing up, Estelle persuaded her friend to run out after him with a piece of paper and a pencil. But she couldn't catch him, though she chased him down the road.

If only she had caught him he would be alive today. Even if he had just slowed the car to give her a wave, if she had delayed him by ten seconds, one second even, Jimmy would have missed the crash and be alive today. Estelle and her friend still got pretty cut-up about it. Too cut-up to come along today, though both were still huge Jimmy fans.

And the Death Drivers sat in the Wendy's and shook their heads over her. Poor kid, she's never forgiven herself. The girl who could have saved James Dean.

Then they would drive on over the mountains to the next spot, seven miles the other side, twenty-two miles south of Bakersfield. It was marked with four silver letters nailed to a telephone pole on the grass strip between the freeway and the little farm road that ran alongside it. The letters spelt DEAN. This was the Ticket Site, and the place for the second big if only . . .

Jimmy was stopped here at 3.30 by a highway patrolman called Oscar Hunter for doing 65 in a 45 zone. The station wagon got a ticket too. I was standing on the verge taking a picture of the spot when a voice behind me said, 'I have a neighbour in the Highway Patrol, he said Oscar Hunter don't blame himself.'

I turned, startled, to find a man in his twenties, with a sharp, Fifties haircut, a white T-shirt, red nylon jacket and blue jeans. He looked like Jimmy's ghost, and next to him stood another guy, dressed exactly like him.

'Well,' said his buddy, 'I guess he don't need to blame himself. He was just doin' his job.'

'Yeah, his wife says he's still pretty cut-up about it though.'

The second if only: if only Oscar Hunter hadn't stopped Jimmy.

It was harvest time and, while I was stopped, a stream of highsided trailers went past, piled full of apples, carrots and other fruit and vegetables. As I put my camera away a truck loaded with grapes came along, its soft, heavy load bouncing gently. As it came level with the telephone pole a bunch of dark grapes the size of a man's head bounced over the side of the truck to fall fifteen feet and splat on the road.

126

A few minutes on up the highway I saw a sign off to the left:

The time is
3.45
Time to buy a Toyota

Or, two hours left for Jimmy.

At Famoso, out the other side of Bakersfield, the Death Drivers turned left onto 46 which was numbered 466 in '55. Dean's final road, where he headed west, through the cotton fields and the peach orchards, into the fatal sunset. It was a ruler-straight road, rolling on for mile after mile, the kind of road that anyone would speed on. They pictured him in that little, loud, low car, feeling every bump of the road, the tiny windscreen keeping only the worst of the hot wind off him, seeing the shimmering water-effect way up ahead that they were seeing now.

It is remote and provincial out here, still a million miles from Hollywood. One autumn day in 1955, there came a rich young man driving a $7,000 sports car, an alien European model that cost more than people out here earned in a year. James Dean – whose only movie seen to date was *East of Eden* – was driving from Hollywood into backwoods America, where he was not yet heard of, let alone famous. A place where you could drive thirty miles and see nothing but cotton; where Wasco, with a population of 9,613 and an old wooden sign that reads 'Wasco – A nice place to live', counts as a big town. Alfred Hitchcock used to commute to L.A. along this road from his home in Santa Cruz, and he captured its air of frightening desolation in the scene in *North by Northwest* in which Cary Grant is pursued by a crop-dusting plane.

A black open-top Porsche appeared in my rear-view mirror, came up close, menacing, before peeling left and zipping past, like a Nineties James Dean. But most on the run did not speed, not on this day, not with the third big 'if only . . .' coming up.

127

At Blackwell's Corner, a seedy truckstop at a remote crossroads ten miles past Lost Hills, where the cotton gives way to desert, James Dean last put his feet on the earth. He stopped at 5 p.m. and spent fifteen minutes here, drank his last Coke and bought a bag of apples.

Jimmy had pulled over because he saw a guy called Lance Reventlow, son of Laura Hutton, who was driving a grey Mercedes 300SL and who was also headed for the race in Salinas.

'If only . . .' If only Jimmy had not spotted that Mercedes, had not pulled over.

Here, those who did not know had to be told that the existing restaurant was further back from the road, and further west, than the one Jimmy stopped at. Look at the square of concrete in front of the two trees, they would tell them. That is the last place where Jimmy stood.

The black Porsche was pulled close into the building, to get what shade it could. The two young guys I had seen in it were leaning against the wall, and drinking milk from cartons. The Dean people went into the truckstop's grocery, maybe sat for a few minutes in one of the plastic booth seats at the far end from the serving counter, beyond all the biscuits and cakes and chips, and the banks of fridges holding the sodas and the beer. Some said Jimmy picked up a six-pack of beer here, but that was a lie, according to the Death Drivers.

They were sore, a couple said to me, at the shape Blackwell's Corner was in. The Mexican guy behind the till seemed to know nothing about Jimmy. Above his head was a sign which read 'Welcome to Blackwell's Corner, James Dean's last . . .' and the rest of it was obscured by a sticker advertising Camel Lites. The rest rooms were disgusting, one of the johns blocked and overflowing, spewing water and such right across the floor.

A middle-aged guy in a check shirt and brown Crimplene pants tucked under his gut, with a little plastic Bart Simpson doll in his hand, went up and stood legs apart, hands on hips, and told him so. But what did the Mexican care, he said, outside once more, and pointing out the exact spot James Dean last stood. What did that guy know about nuthin'? 'This place should be a national monument,' he said. 'Last spot where Jimmy's feet touched America.'

Then they moved on out for the final twenty-six miles, arranging to meet up 900 yards past the death site, at Jack's Ranch Café, where there is a shining chrome memorial to Jimmy. 'Keep it slow guys,' called one. 'Keep to the speed limit. Like Jimmy did.'

Then they were each alone with their thoughts of Jimmy as they drove those final miles, the baking hot sun low before their eyes, desert on either side, the black funeral ribbon of road unrolling ahead. On the brow of a hill a green 1955 Austin Healey which had passed me just after Blackwell's was at the side of the road, the driver flagging me down. He had run out of gas. I took his companion, a teenager named Jason, on to the monument, where he had his own car parked, and could go and get petrol for the Healey. Jason said he had just met the other guy at Cholame, they had taken a zip up to Blackwell's, and were headed back.

At the monument a dumpy little guy called Ralph Delisio was standing by his Cavalier clutching a white plastic ring binder. On the front, in red sticky-back capitals it said:

JD
HWY 46-41
1955-1985
Sept 30
HERE BEGAN
THE LEGEND

Ralph told me he knew more about the crash than anyone else alive, and announced we were an hour ahead of time.

How come, Ralph?

Because, he said, daylight saving was not in operation on 30 September 1955, but it was today. It came off on 26 September in '55. He had checked up in the records at the Griffith Observatory in Hollywood, that place which plays such a central role in *Rebel Without a Cause*, the film which would be released three days after Jimmy's death.

With the clocks set as they were today, the time of Jimmy's crash was actually 6.45, not 5.45, said Ralph. Couldn't we see, the sun was not about to set, the conditions were not the same. We had an hour to chew the fat about Jimmy before we need head back to the crash site. Set your watches.

In the middle of the parking lot beside the café stands a tree, and around the tree has been built a memorial to James Dean. It is a modern, angular affair which encloses the tree on two sides at ground level, then rises to six feet to run round the other two sides. It looks like the entrance sign to an industrial park. It bears the wording:

James Dean
1931 Feb 8 – 1955 Sept 30 pm 5:59

But 5.59 p.m. is the time of the emergency call to the Highway Patrol. The actual time of the crash is a matter of dispute, because from it can be determined his average speed since he got his parking ticket, and it has a bearing on whether or not he was speeding at the fatal moment. Those who favour Dean's image as a fearless, reckless, dare-devil rebel put it as early as 5.30, they talk with admiration of his zipping down into the Cholame valley at 100, even 130 m.p.h. It was one of these people, presumably, who scratched into the chrome centrepiece the slogan: 'Live fast, die young, and have a good-looking corpse,' from Nicholas Ray's *Knock on Any Door*, which Jimmy himself was fond of quoting. The rest, who are by far the majority in this gathering, go for 5.45, and claim he was well within the speed limit. The inquest put his speed at 86, but no-one seems to have much faith in the inquest.

The Death Drivers know the vital statistics of this cenotaph. 'Cost $200,000,' murmured one to me as I stood reading the inscription. 'Put it up in '83. Weighs 120 tons. Japanese guy name of Seita Ohnishi paid for it.'

Around the centrepiece was an area covered with large round stones, and then a concrete wall partly topped with hefty wooden beams, from which, the expert told me, little James Dean medallions had been prised by souvenir-hunters. They took the stones too, which had been brought from Japan. But in the café they had bags of the things, and when they got low out here they put more out.

There were official quotations on the monument as well: 'What is essential is invisible to the eye' – Antoine de Saint-Exupéry, and, from Mr Ohnishi: 'In Japan we say that his death came as suddenly as it does to cherry blossoms. The petals of early spring always fall at the height of their ephemeral brilliance.'

There was a plaque set against the concrete wall with another much longer inscription from Mr Ohnishi. It began: 'A small token – this monument stands as a small token of my appreciation for the people of America from whom I have learned so much. It celebrates a people who have over the years cour- ageously followed the path of truth and justice while expanding the limits of mankind with their boundless pioneering spirit. It also stands for James Dean and other American rebels who taught us the importance of having a cause. For all those who helped this stranger from Japan realise his dream of erecting this monument I express my heartfelt thanks,' and ended: 'In gratitude to all the James Dean fans who have carried his torch throughout the years.'

Ohnishi had intrigued me ever since I learned about his gift of the monument. I had imagined he was a

Japanese-American, but he is not. He lives in Tokyo, speaks no English, and is contactable via a representative in San Francisco. I had tried to interview him, or even his representative, but in the end had to settle for faxing off a long list of written questions. When the answers came back, many of the questions had been ignored. 'Mr Ohnishi is a shy man,' said the representative apologetically. All Ohnishi's answers told me was that he became a fan of Dean when he saw *East of Eden* in 1956, that he did not study Dean's life or collect material on him – though Ralph Delisio claimed Ohnishi owns the only pictures of Dean taken in the car after the crash and paid $250,000 to Sanford Roth's widow for all prints and negatives. Dean was popular in Japan, Ohnishi said, because 'It is an intrinsic aspect of Japanese culture to mourn the premature passing of truly talented young men and to always hold their memory dear. In Japan, and worldwide, James Dean is seen as so talented that he should have been immortalized with an Academy Award.' Ohnishi said he had decided to erect the monument because 'In 1976, I learned that it was not easy to locate the site of his death.'

I watched the crowd gather at the monument. There were now six lookalikes, fiddling with their props: putting their sunglasses on and taking them off again; taking unlit cigarettes from behind their ears, slotting them between their lips, holding them between their fingers, but never lighting them. They took it in turns to photograph each other leaning against the memorial.

There was an air of expectation. Madonna had shown up one year, I heard, when she was with Sean Penn. Dennis Hopper, he'd been there. The guy who gave Dean the speeding ticket had come along once, but hadn't revealed who he was. He'd told a friend afterwards that he had enjoyed himself, that the Dean fans were a nice bunch of people. Ohnishi himself was said to come along too occasionally.

There was a Japanese man with a camcorder and a

beany hat moving quietly around, videoing the monument. I had just said hello to him and was about to ask
him who he was when a bunch of college kids in a
battered blue Chrysler with a buckled wing skidded to
a halt right in front of us. A loudmouth with black hair
and an ear stud came up to us shouting and waving two
bottles of Andre champagne, a marque that was new
to me. 'God!' he yelled in our faces. 'Unreal! I can't
believe it! The master, drink to the master! Oh boy,
Jimmy! God, I've waited all my life for this moment.'
The Japanese bolted for his Nissan as the loudmouth
turned on one of the lookalikes: 'Hey dude, where you
from? L.A.? Me too, where you at school?'

There was another guy in the car, plus a fat brunette
and a cutesy little blonde with bubbly hair. They began
scattering dried flowers over Ohnishi's plaque and
trailing a length of black ribbon, stolen from a cemetery
for this very purpose, from the branches of the tree.

A woman called Bobbi, in purple shorts and pink
socks, placed a bunch of red roses on the memorial.
She then took from her car a container of blue detergent
and a cloth and began polishing up the monument, a
little self-conscious in front of these loud teenagers. I
told her she was really making it gleam in the low
autumn sun and she said she liked to keep it neat.
There were crazies who damaged it now and then,
once someone blasted it with a shotgun. She collected
the empty Andre bottles and placed them in a rubbish
drum.

There was a guy who said his name was Mark
Deaver, who lived in Fairmount Apartments, Van Nuys
('and where did Dean come from? Fairmount, Indiana,
right?'). He told me he had written a movie script about
the Dean crash which the sons of a gun at Warner
Brothers had rejected, then put out almost the selfsame
movie as *Back to the Future*. Did I remember that film?
Well, he said, in his version the guy wanted to go back
to 1955 in a De Lorean to catch up with James Dean
before he was killed. He wanted to show him that his

car was faster, he would stop Dean on the highway and say hey, want my car? And if necessary he would go on in the Porsche and get himself killed, to spare Jimmy.

Then from the west came the Spitfire roar of a Porsche Spyder, a kit-car replica of Jimmy's car, the same in every way, except that it did not have the race number 130 that Jimmy had, nor the nickname Little Bastard painted on it. People gathered to take its picture with the memorial in the background.

At 6.30, or 5.30 as Ralph insisted we should think of it, the cars began to slip off, the Spyder zipping ahead, going back up 46 to the junction with 41 – the crash site. When I got there Ralph Delisio was standing with his white book open, everyone else crowded around him. The Spyder was not parked up with the rest of the cars.

The professor of Dean-crash-ology, his camcorder-toting wife and mother-in-law in tow, was propounding his theory that far from speeding when he crashed, Dean was only travelling at 45, maybe 40.

Ralph was saying: 'I first came out here on the anniversary in 1970, and I took one look at this spot and I said to myself, "Well I think you really got the railroad job Jimmy, you got stabbed in the back, there is no way you caused that crash."'

Oh yeah, Ralph, how come?

'Look,' he said, 'look at all this documentation I got here, then do a simple sum.'

He flipped over the clear plastic pouches in his ring binder. He showed us a copy of the speeding ticket, timed at 3.30. Could we all see that? We could. It took five minutes to write the ticket, he said. Then he showed us a copy of the death certificate. It put the time of the crash at 5.45. He had a copy of the Highway Patrol accident report, which also put the time of the crash at 5.45.

An insect landed on Ralph's back. His mother-in-law, in her camel coat, hands clasped over a black patent handbag, stared at it for a second, then reached up and brushed it away. Ralph was not distracted.

'So, here comes the sum,' he said. 'Jimmy got the ticket at 3.30, the accident was at 5.45, that's two hours and fifteen minutes, that'll give you 120, plus 15, that's 135 minutes to go the 108 miles from ticket site to crash site. And they stopped once, for ten minutes, at Blackwell's Corner. So that's 125 minutes to go 108 miles, which is less than 60 m.p.h.

'It's on paper,' said Ralph as we digested this evidence, 'written by the pros. They were there.'

He gave us another, subsidiary sum. Say they left Blackwell's at eight after five. That gave you thirty-seven minutes to go twenty-six miles. 'There is no way he was speeding, it is impossible, it can't be done.'

Someone held up a sign to the traffic: 'Honk if Dean lives'. A lot of the cars did. A truck loaded with garlic went past, filling the air with a brief pungency.

Ralph said it had taken him twenty years to solve to his satisfaction the question of blame in the crash. First he had had to get hold of copies of the crash photographs taken by Highway Patrolman Ron Nelson. Boy, that had been a tough one. Then, he had come out and taken his own photographs, lining them up on trees, buildings, a water tower, so that he could recreate the exact locations from which Nelson took his photographs and identify where everything happened on the new road alignments which had been made since '55.

He flipped through the eerie black and white shots, taken as the gloom deepened over the desert, which showed the Ford, driven by a twenty-three-year-old student called Donald Turnupseed, crumpled on one wing and spun around. They showed the Porsche crushed, said Ralph, like a Pepsi can, all down one side, and come to rest against a telegraph pole. The pole was long gone, but if we started at this water culvert and paced out 115 feet this way, and then 45 feet this way, we were right on the money, right on the button.

So then you could determine the distance between the point of impact and the point at which the Porsche came to rest. And, said Ralph, there was no way that, if Jimmy had been doing 86, he could have come to a stop in such a short space. There were no skid marks from Jimmy.

And in any case, he said, Turnupseed was turning left at a junction, crossing Jimmy's path. In that situation the car in Jimmy's position had the right of way. That was the law. He had us all convinced.

The blonde got out of the car, wiggling across, walking with her toes clawed to keep her clogs on, and said to the loudmouth, 'Are we gonna sit out here all night?'

Her boyfriend brushed her away. 'So how come everyone says he was speeding?' he asked Ralph.

'Well,' he said, 'I been giving that a lot of thought. Look at it like this. Dean is a rich Hollywood kid. He never went in the military, never married, didn't have any kids. Turnupseed is a Navy vet, his wife was pregnant at the time, he didn't have any money. World War Two was only ten years before, Korea barely over, so a lot of people looked on Dean as he had it all, this guy doesn't have anything. It was just an accident, these things happen.

'Every book I read, it upsets the hell out of me. They say Dean was a maniac and he was out there speeding at 86 and nobody does any research at all. What they are saying is impossible. Dean used to go to the cemetery when he was nine years old, after his mother died, and he stood at her grave and he said, "I'm going to be a success, I'm going to make it without you." And he had just made it. Why in the hell would he want to commit suicide?'

The air cooled, the sun tipped behind the hills to the east, shadows grew as you watched them. As the minutes ticked by to the fateful time, Ralph said he had one last thing to show us. He passed round a green slip of card with a lot of printing on it and the signature, D. Turnupseed. Ralph, who was a postman, told us it was a receipt which proved that a certified letter had been received by the person it was intended for.

'Look at that signature,' he said. 'The guy who killed James Dean!'

There were suitable murmurs.

'Want to know how I got it?'

It seemed Ralph had seen that Turnupseed's electrical company, based seventy miles north-east of here in Tulare, had placed an ad in a Hollywood newspaper for companies that wished to do business with it to get in touch. Ralph had gone to the secretary of an electrical company on his delivery round and asked if they would respond to Turnupseed's ad. They did, and Ralph said, 'Better send it certified, make sure he gets it. I'll pay, I'll take it to the post office.'

Then, armed with the letter, Ralph went up to Tulare and sat outside Turnupseed Electric, 1580 South K, waiting for the regular postman to come along. It was the afternoon before he stopped by.

'This your regular time around here?' Ralph asked him, showing his government licence. It was.

So, next day, Ralph turned up at 9.30 a.m. At about a quarter to ten Turnupseed's Corvette turned into the premises. Ten minutes later Ralph went in.

'"Got a certified letter for Donald Turnupseed. Need his signature."

'A big doofy-lookin' guy comes out. Like a big Benny Hill. Close as I am to you. Big stoopid-lookin' idiot. Boy, I'd wanted to see what he looked like for twenty-two years. I thought, fella, I'd like to get you out in the car and ask you a few questions.' He took back the green card and looked at it again, shaking his head, saying, 'Donald Turnupseed, the man who killed James Dean,' as if he still couldn't believe it.

'I wanted to throw a few things at him, but I didn't, I didn't push it. Because he's never talked about it and he won't. If someone won't talk about something they are guilty. It took all my strength not to say something. And I was worried about the regular coming in at the wrong time. But I didn't do anything wrong, I didn't go in there and try to intimidate the guy or anything else. The yellow slip went back to the post office, so they got that on record.

'A police handwriting expert analysed the signature for me. He said "Very insecure, paranoic, incapable of completing anything, unreliable, and prone to lie quite often."

'Now what I'd like to do, they have a store in Beverly Hills has James Dean autographs, and they are like $4,000, $6,000, $12,000. If I took this up there and said, "Hey, this is the guy that killed him, how much is this worth?" Maybe they could put it together with one of Jimmy's. But I wouldn't sell it.'

Ralph conceded that Turnupseed had had a lot to live with, perpetually under the cloud of having killed James Dean. He'd had fans go into his office and try to jump him, he'd had graffiti painted on his walls: James Dean lives.

The first cars with headlights on came down Jimmy's last hill. The blonde said, 'God, this is a beautiful spot to die.'

And then it started to happen. The countdown, the Spyder going past, and it was magical for a moment, before reality clicked back in and it was just the Porsche replica zipping through.

The Death Drivers began to move off back to their cars. As they did Ralph was saying, 'Look at it like this. Every single day for the next million years, we'll get in a car. You get in a car in Hollywood, you leave at 12.30, and you drive out to Cholame. I'll get in a car in Cal Poly, San Luis Obispo, and I'll drive to Cholame. I'll leave at four when Turnupseed left. You know how many times we are going to come together exactly at that intersection so we could hit? In a million years? 365 million times? Not once. Not once.'

But while Ralph was obsessed by the mechanics of the crash, I was thinking of what it did to James Dean's power over my imagination, and the imaginations of all the other millions who were in his thrall.

Jimmy was the first teenager, the first public representation of independent, rebellious, fun-loving youth. Turnupseed represented staid, crusty, good-old-boy America. The latter killed the former. But Dean's death was just what the emerging youth cult needed to fire it up into an all-consuming conflagration. Three days after his death, *Rebel Without a Cause* was released, to scenes of mass hysteria. His death was the best possible publicity for the film. As teenagers watched it, they were watching Jimmy's epitaph: his fate was inseparable from the movie and how it was received.

Dean plays an adolescent looking for identity, love from his parents and the friendship of his peers. Because he is always getting into trouble his parents have moved him from town to town. He ends up in Los Angeles, where his interest in a schoolgirl, played by Natalie Wood, gets him into a knife fight with her leather-jacketed boyfriend. Dean wins but is challenged to a chicken run. He and his rival will drive stolen cars towards the edge of a cliff. The first one to jump from his car is a chicken. Dean survives but the other boy dies. The film climaxes with Dean trying to intervene on behalf of another classmate, a disturbed, neglected rich kid played by Sal Mineo, who is eventually killed in an armed stand-off with the police.

It is not the plot that gives the film its power, but Dean's portrayal of a teenager who is made rebellious by the neglect of his parents and what he sees as the alien and oppressive nature of adult society.

Many put Dean's – and *Rebel*'s – appeal down to all the things that terrified them about the young. They were wrong. François Truffaut got it right when he said of him, 'In James Dean, today's youth discovers itself. Less for the reasons usually advanced: violence, sadism, hysteria, pessimism, cruelty and filth, than for others infinitely more simple and commonplace: modesty of feeling, continual fantasy life, moral purity without relation to everyday morality but all the more rigorous, eternal adolescent love of tests and trials, intoxication, pride, and regret at feeling oneself "outside" society, refusal and desire to become integrated and, finally, acceptance – or refusal – of the world as it is.'

Rebel was the ultimate teen anthem. It still is. Because Jimmy died young and beautiful he will live for ever, and so will the film. If he were alive today, a man in his sixties, he would be no more important than Marlon Brando, whose rebel biker image in *On the Waterfront* could have become as powerful as Dean's in *Rebel*, but was erased because he lived on to get old and make junk. As I was saying at the beginning: if you want to live for ever . . . die young.

CHAPTER EIGHT

Any Friend of Jimmy's . . .

JAMES DEAN,
FAIRMOUNT, INDIANA, OCTOBER

Adeline Nall was stumbling through the memories. Trying to build a picture. Only last evening there had been someone, another visitor. Yes, a girl, here to talk to her about her Jim Dean. Like they all were.

'She gave me a book. I got a book last night. Where is it?' With stiff fingers she went through the large cardboard box on the floor beside her armchair, stuffed with papers and stamped '60 Depend Underguard Extra Absorbent'.

'Di somebody,' she said, still searching. 'I thought it was here. No. Well it's someplace around here. It's a trial to find anything. Di what's her name? I can't think of it.' She moved carefully, awkwardly to another pile of papers on the windowsill. 'I read it last night right after she gave it to me. Do you see it? Can't remember what it was called. Ah! I remember the girl's name. It was Di Eldon.'

A terrible racking cough came from a resident in another room somewhere down the long, wide corridor of the nursing home.

'It's poetry,' Adeline went on, the memory forming but the book remaining obstinately invisible. 'No rhyme to it. She's hunting Jim sort of thing and she finds him and she loves him and she expects him to love her in return. I get a lot of people who write to me like that.'

I asked her whether she thought they might be mentally ill?

An alarm sounded somewhere down the corridor, an insistent electronic beep.

'No,' she replied. 'They are not. She was an interesting girl. She had pants on. She was tall and she had a sweater and a coat. The coat was long.'

The beeping alarm persisted, unanswered.

Adeline told me about the James Dean fans who seek her out, drawn to the woman who taught him speech and drama at high school. It was she who enabled him to focus his energy and amazing powers of concentration on something – on acting, as it happened – and thereby helped to create the James Dean that we knew. Adeline was still keeping his memory alive with her annual memorial services and willingness to welcome admirers and to talk.

'They know he is dead,' said Adeline. 'But they love the boy. Di Eldon loves the boy. They do, they really love him. He was a sweet boy, he was. He didn't hold grudges. There was a new principal in school. He was a big man. He picked on me for having no discipline. Well, he didn't know whether I did or didn't.'

Along the corridor a nurse had come in answer to the alarm. 'What is it Beth, honey?' she asked. 'Ice water? Sure honey, I'll bring you some ice water.' She walked past the open door to get it, smiling in at us.

Adeline struggled with the story, the story she loves to tell, from the days when she had Jim Dean in her class in the little red-brick castle of a school in Fairmount, Indiana. Her class consisted of just ten pupils, seven boys and three girls, and Jim Dean the star among them. Jim was preparing for a state-wide speech contest by declaiming a Dickensian monologue about a madman. A boy was goading Dean as he spoke, until it nearly got to a fight. And then the bell rang which defused the situation, but Dean and this other boy – what was his name? – had met at the door. There had been words, then a scuffle on the stairs and the booming voice of the principal who had been at the bottom of the flight listening, watching, waiting for the fracas that would show that Adeline Nall could not keep order.

But the story proved too hard to tell for the little old lady, frail as a bird, in her green satin pyjamas with the big pink flouncy bow on one shoulder that made her look gift-wrapped.

She gave up and came back to the present.

'I'm surprised so many people come here. People really admire him. They love him. They do. It's kind of pitiful that people have to love somebody they do not know – that they have to have somebody to hang onto.'

And still they come to find her, even though she is eighty-seven now, crippled with Parkinson's and in this nursing home. They come to touch someone who was close to James Dean.

I was another one who had sought her out at the Flinn nursing home, on 14th street in Marion. I had walked down the wide corridors lined with strips of polished wood at stretcher height, corridors dotted with shrunken forms struggling to propel themselves in wheelchairs, past the confused old woman in the doorway of her room calling feebly, 'Help me sonny, help me please, just a little.' I had gone through the recreation room with its giant TV screen, with the wheelchairs pulled up to it like a disabled drive-in. Through the chapel, past the soiled-laundry room to Adeline Nall in 312.

And didn't Adeline love Jimmy too?

'I loved Jimmy, yes, but differently. My son was two years younger and I had to be careful not to say too much about Jim before David.'

Mentioning David brought her back to the story she had been trying to tell me, of Jimmy's speech contest. It had been rehearsing that monologue which had led to the fight.

She talked of that proudest of proud days, 8 April

143

1949 – there, she remembered it still – when her son David was competing in a state-wide Future Farmers of America public speaking contest. Jim Dean picked Adeline up and drove her to the little town of Peru, to this other contest that he was in, being held at Peru High School. And both won! Adeline was ecstatic: mother to one, teacher to the other. Then she and Jim had to go together to the national contest, on a train all the way to Longmont, Colorado. What a send-off they had had, the band and cheerleaders on the lawns before the high school. In Colorado Jim got through to the semi-finals, despite going over the ten-minute time limit, but that night when Adeline went looking for him to make sure he practised, concentrated on the semi-finals the next day, she could not find him. Jimmy had goofed off. And at the semi-finals he went over time again and lost.

'I can see him still, sitting crumpled up in his seat during the finals. He was heartsick. Jim blamed me for it. Well, there you go, you can't win.' Adeline seemed struck by the sudden clarity of the memory. Her little elfin face broke into a beam behind her large glasses. 'How strange,' she said, 'I haven't thought of that in an age.

'Jimmy and I were close. I lost my father when I was twelve years old, Jim Dean lost his mother when he was nine, so our lives kind of went together. We had things in common I suppose.'

Adeline told me she was born in Marion in 1906 to a Quaker family called Mart, went to Chicago after school to teach, and married a young social worker called Darl Nall. They had David but then the marriage collapsed and she returned to Indiana, first to Marion, then to Fairmount in 1940. This was the year Jimmy came back after his mother's death from cancer in California.

'After Jimmy graduated we stayed in touch. He was acting in New York, then in California but he'd come back through Fairmount pretty regularly and I'd get a call.'

She told me the story of how James Dean inspired her, encouraged her, to throw up schoolteaching and go to New York to become an actress. 'Maybe it seems foolish,' she said, 'I was a middle-aged woman with a marriage and twenty-two years of schoolteaching behind me, and I went to Broadway. And I did it, I became an actress. I went to New York in 1953 and saw Jimmy rehearsing for a play and that started me wondering whether I could do it too.'

The play was called *The Immoralist*, which Jimmy left to make his first film, *East of Eden*.

But it took another two years for Adeline to up sticks and go to New York, after the last visit Jimmy would make to Fairmount, in February 1955. He came with a photographer from *Life* magazine called Dennis Stock, who took some memorable, definitive pictures of Jimmy, at the Sweetheart Ball, walking downtown, and out on the farm. This time she didn't get a call, and worried that she had offended him in some way, or that he had become too grand to bother with his old high-school teacher. 'It kept eating at me,' she said. 'So finally I drove over to the house. Turned out he was not mad at me, just preoccupied with being a star all of a sudden and having people follow him around and I told him he had to put up with that, being considerate to people who are attracted to you is part of being a star. The last words I ever spoke to him were "Don't forget to be kind."'

'Jimmy set me on a whole new career. I just was fed-up with what I had, the same kids, the same school, the same town. I had only been in New York nine weeks when I learned he had been killed.'

On the morning of Saturday 1 October she was working at the desk of a hotel called the Biltmore. The manager, who knew of her friendship, phoned Adeline to tell her he had just read it in the *New York Times*.

'I wanted to stay on because I had given up my job and the girl who had taken it was a former pupil of mine. And so I stayed and they gave me a year's contract and then extended it another year. I was just beginning to get my foot in the door at the end of the second year. I did a play off Broadway and had fun doing it, but somehow it stopped working out, it didn't seem right.

'Then I came back here, and I taught again, until 1972. Jimmy has occupied a lot of my life since I returned, there isn't a day when I don't think about him or talk about him to someone.'

The story had ended but the memories were still spinning round in her head, little bits of them surfacing in speech now as she tired, little disjointed thoughts: 'The principal. No discipline. They fought on the stairs. The speech contest. Ran over. Jim blamed me. I did wrong. I did something wrong. What did I do wrong? Can't remember.' Adeline's voice got quieter and quieter. 'I'm getting tired, I've been talking too much.'

She asked me to sign her visitors' book and when we had found it I did. As I finished writing I looked over to her in the armchair. Her eyelids were heavy, her head lolling back. I closed the book and left.

The night before I had landed at Chicago, flying in from Los Angeles a few days after the anniversary of James Dean's death to find out what his home town could tell me about him. I had driven as far as Kokomo that night, approaching Fairmount across the Indiana countryside, a blood-orange sunset behind me, a smell from the cooling earth like Greek coffee, earthy, dusty and sweet. I was tired and stopped the night in a motel swarming with kids and built around an indoor swimming-pool that filled the place with the smell of chlorinated water. When the kids weren't in the pool they were in the lifts with their wet hair, pushing all the buttons, riding up and down all evening.

I awoke next day to pick up my journey in the cool of a Sunday morning. Fairmount lies in wide-open country. The town is a clearing in the fields, a people circle in an ocean of corn: a haven in the crops for those who tend them.

I sped east over the flatlands on Indiana 26, the cool morning turning into a bright autumn day. Every couple of miles the crops parted for a hamlet, each hamlet dominated by the silver-cylinder clusters of grain silos and a church, like the Southview Assembly of God, a huge modern barn of a place in beige metal, distinguished from the other barns around it by the ten-foot white cross on the gable end. It was a vast new church, big enough for the factory-farming of souls, with a roadside notice-board bearing the slogan: 'Thank you Lord for that secret place where we meet you'.

Outside the wooden shacks, beneath the shade of oaks, men leant against pick-ups, scratching themselves awake. In the farmyards, posses of six-wheel tractors with elongated red bonnets were gathering. I passed through Hemlock where Hemlock Friends Church promised 'All new sermons, no reruns', through Phlox with its beautiful Dutch barns, through a place called West Liberty – as if liberty had a geography – where a farm had a lifesize tableau of a brown and white sow and six piglets standing on a brick platform beside the road.

And then came a big white metal arrow at a T-junction: Fairmount one mile, then a sign saying 'Fairmount – home town of James Byron Dean'. The road entered town between clipped verges and pastel-painted houses. Church bells were chiming. It dipped beneath maples just losing their leaves, past the fire station and the pale blue water tower, rising gently to the stop light where Washington crosses Main, pinpointing Fairmount.

I recognize this intersection from a Dennis Stock photograph which has Jimmy in farmhand's clothing, smoking a cigarette and walking down Washington towards the house which is now the museum that contains so many of his things.

147

In the time it took to park and get out of the car my eye took in all the town had to offer. There was a cop car outside the Memories Diner, which was open. Just beyond it was the Palace Bar – its reinforced metal door shut – which ceased to be the Palace Cinema before James Dean had made a film. The record store offered 'Dean Dylan Clash $3.99' posters. There was an old painted sign on an end wall for Gold Medal Flour, a barber's shop, Fairmount PRO hardware, Napa auto parts, a launderette at the far end of the street before the road dipped under the maples and away out of town. No-one was about, but a pick-up coasted past.

In the time, also, that it took to park and get out I could run through the complete history of Fairmount. The white man came in 1823, having stumbled across the shady place beside the river he named Back Creek by following the Indian trails that led the pioneers west. The first settler was Joseph Winslow. Jimmy's mother was a Winslow. Joseph Winslow cleared land four miles north of town where the Marcus Winslow farm now stands. After his mother died this was where Jimmy was brought and where he grew up, cared for by his aunt and uncle, Hortense and Marcus Winslow.

Jim Dean was born in Marion, the 40,000-strong town ten miles north. He was taken to California as a small boy because his father, a dental technician, was offered a better job in a hospital in Los Angeles. There his mother died from cancer and his father, feeling unable to raise Jimmy alone, sent him to his relations in Fairmount, gave him to the embrace and comfort of his family. He grew, secure in the clutch of this small town, grew among friends and those who loved him, grew until by some miracle he became that strangest of strange new things: the first teenager.

Today the little town is famous for James Dean, direct descendant of the man who founded the place. In late September, while I was standing in the desert with one bunch of fans, another, huge group – 30,000- to 40,000-strong – had come here for three days of Dean activities, a veteran-car show and lookalike contests. They filled all the motels for sixty miles around, visited the museum and the James Dean gallery, which houses the largest collection of Dean memorabilia in the world, visited his grave and the Winslow farmyard.

If I followed the footsteps Jim Dean took in Dennis Stock's photograph, put the Citizen's bank behind me and walked a block down silent, sunny Washington I would come to the town museum, which is a collectively-built, homely memorial to James Dean. His family, friends and contemporaries have turned out their cupboards and bottom drawers, their scrap-books and photo albums, and created an incredibly detailed record of his life and his relationship with all of them.

Walking around, it seemed as if everything Jimmy had ever owned was here. Everything from his baby clothes and his Bible to pictures of himself with his father Winton and grandfather Charlie Dean, from his address book with numbers for Liz Taylor, Hedda Hopper, Exterminator and Jack's Cleaners, to souvenirs of his love of sports-car racing.

It all adds up to a multi-stranded weaving of a small-town life, the overwhelming evidence that the people here loved him so much, and had loved him long before he was famous, that they had kept all these things to remember him by. It was presided over now by Jim's great buddy, Bob Pulley, who played ice hockey with him on the frozen pond at the farm, who went partying with him in the bars of Marion, who was one of his pall-bearers, and who now looks after his memory here. Bob walked around the showcases with me.

He had his favourites: 'This is his old electric train. When Marky [Jimmy's cousin Marcus] brought it in, wa'n't no wheels on the back of that caboose. I had one similar so I took the wheels off my train, put them right on here.' Next to the train were a cup and saucer, the cup inscribed The Challenger, and a photograph. 'When they brought his mother back from California they came on a train called the Challenger. Jimmy wanted a souvenir from the train that brought his mommy home and that's what he was given.'

Bob was a little guy, wiry, in grey polyester slacks and a pale blue and yellow polo shirt, with thin grey hair and watery blue eyes behind his glasses. Strange how you expect the contemporaries of the eternal teenager to be eternally young themselves.

Because he had known Dean so well, Bob's presence made this a living museum to Jimmy.

'It was a kind of shock to the town when Jimmy was killed. Jim was home in February of '55 and I was even hesitant to call him then because I thought well he's big-time now, he's too good for us. But I was wrong. It tickled him that someone from home remembered him. So he said what do we do so I said well party I guess. So we did. We went off to a tavern in Marion and had a wild old time. Jimmy had a trick of filling his mouth with lighter fuel then getting a match and striking it then spraying the gas out in a burst of flame.' He shook his head at the memory. 'But there were some was jealous of him. There was an older man that night in the tavern and he said "Hey you didn't give me your autograph", well Jim did and he tore it up right in front of us.

'I went out to the farm the next day before he left to go back and that's the last time I ever got to see him. He wrote his address down for me, he wanted me to go out to see him but he got killed before I got a chance. I think he wanted someone from here to just go out and see how things were in Hollywood. He was proud of hisself which I don't blame him for.

'He didn't talk too much about the movies, he talked about his love life more, like he was crazy about a girl called Pier Angeli, but she went off and married Vic Damone. He was really broke up over that, I do remember him talking about that.'

When Pier, whom Dean met on *East of Eden*, and

150

Damone, the singer, married at St Timothy's Catholic Church, Dean sat across the road on his motorcycle, gunning the engine as bride and groom emerged after the service.

Bob has become a focus for many of the people who want to know more about James Dean, particularly kids. 'He's had so much effect on even younger kids, I'm talking twelve and thirteen. Every time there is something on TV which I'm part of, why I start getting mail from these kids. They are just fascinated, they ask things about Jimmy. I try and acknowledge every letter I get, probably four or five a day, right through the year – that's personal mail, not the mail we get here at the museum.

'It's a full-time occupation, I can be up until one or two in the morning answering letters, but if it will help some kid why then I'm happy to do it.

'*Rebel* is the one that these kids relate to. My favourite is *East of Eden*. That's closest to what he was like on the farm. I had a girl who was twelve years old she said her parents were having problems, she'd seen *Rebel* and she wanted to be just like Jimmy. I turned round and explained that she needed to get things sorted out with her parents, and I explained to her that this was just Jimmy acting, he wasn't really that type of person. Best way to describe Jimmy, he was a normal boy. He wa'n't any different than any other kid. He was ambitious and he was talented. Whatever he wanted to do – his painting, his track records, football, basketball – he wanted to do well. We'd be playing ice hockey out at the farm and we'd take a break and we'd always have a fire going to keep warm. We'd all go and stand by the fire and talk a bit but Jim, he'd be out there practising. Not to be better than we were but to be better himself. He was just always pushing himself.'

Bob broke off when we heard the door to the museum open and women's voices. He went and sold them their tickets while I continued to look around the walls. I could hear him asking where y'all from and a woman saying going east to Pittsburgh, come from Kansas City . . . separated from my husband . . . going with my daughter here to Pittsburgh to stay with my sister for a while . . . got a job lined up . . . telling Bob Pulley her life story. Bob said and this is your daughter? Yes, this is Velvet.

'Velvet. Pretty name.'

Then he came back through and found me looking at Jimmy's Triumph motorcycle.

'It's amazing that folks have kept so many things. I've kept everything that I had through school and I'm glad I did. We all went to Washington with the track teams and I've even got the bars of soap in their wrappers and stationery from the hotels we stayed in. Just things like that. The wife found a little book from high school the other day, it is kind of a memories book of my senior year. Jimmy had signed two pages. A lot of people kept things. We didn't know at the time he was going anywhere. I just did it for myself.'

The mother and daughter came into the room. She had big hair, leggings and a shoulder bag, her daughter was blonde, in stretch jeans and white boots.

Bob was saying, 'Jim would be from February to August older than me. It was kind of sad just seeing him in February, next thing you know he's gone. But that's life. There's not been many like Jim, maybe Elvis Presley, and maybe Marilyn Monroe, the three of them, just legends the three of them.'

The woman, whose name I discovered later was Tammi, was listening to this, her mouth dropping open. 'Did you KNOW Jimmy Dean?' she asked.

Bob said sure he did, they had been good friends. Tammi tried to impress her daughter, who must have been about fourteen, with this piece of living history, but if she was interested she was too shy to acknowledge as much.

Bob and I moved out and stood on the porch where he told me about the other person who, along

152

with Adeline Nall, had done a great deal to shape Jim. He was a Wesleyan pastor called Dr James de Weerd, a boy's man, a war hero, an individualist who opened youngsters up to adventure, the arts, ambition, things that took them beyond the confines of a small town and its possibilities. It is often said that de Weerd opened Jimmy's mind while Adeline focused his energies on acting. He taught Dean to drive and in his senior year took him to the Indianapolis 500. He encouraged him to have no fear of death, to believe in personal immortality.

'He was kind of a father to most of us boys,' said Bob. 'He'd take a bunch of us swimming – that was back at the Y when you'd swim in the nude. He'd take a whole groups of us boys down and he'd bring us back to his house and maybe fix us something to eat and we'd play records and then he'd see we all got home. He just kind of looked over us, till he got married. He was real broad-minded. This was back when women weren't supposed to wear slacks and he would sit in front of the church till about five minutes before his sermon started and watch people going in. One night I was with him sitting out front and this lady walked down the street dressed in slacks and Jim said Bob, if she walks in that church I'll preach them slacks right off her.'

I asked Bob about Jimmy's family and whether any of them were still around and he said sure, Jimmy's cousin Marcus – whom he called Marky – still lived out at the Winslow farm where Jimmy was brought up. He telephoned him for me and Marky said send him right on out.

So I drove north on Sand Pike, past the cemetery where Jimmy is buried, past the Back Creek Friends Church, the Winslow family church, where Adeline Nall's memorial services take place. A mile on there is a bend in the road and then the farmhouse, a two-storey frame house on a stone foundation, painted a pristine white, with a wide porch with a swing bench suspended on chains from the roof, the house surrounded by oaks and sycamores.

At the farm I went up to the side porch, to be met at the screen door by Marcus Winslow. We went into the room directly behind this door. Inside, the house had cool white walls and unpainted oak doors – it felt plain and honest and simple. Marcus was wearing a red and blue check shirt and sitting on a red and blue check chair, into which I could make him dissolve if I let my focus soften. He shared the Winslow build with Jimmy Dean. If Jimmy had been allowed to get old and thicken out he would look pretty much like Marcus did now.

Ever since 1955 people have been coming out to this farm, to touch the memory. It is now a long time since they would have found Marcus and Hortense, the aunt and uncle who brought Jim Dean up, still living on this farm, a long time since the days when all of his belongings remained in his room on the first floor just as he had left them. The Winslows have welcomed hundreds, thousands of people over the years, letting them camp on their meadows, occasionally letting them stay in his room, like the sailor turned Buddhist who slept in Jimmy's room and chanted at his grave.

To all of them they explained that Jim was just an ordinary boy, not a rebel, not eaten up with anger or hate or whatever, just an all-round home-town-loving boy who had a talent that he worked on and made a success of himself through. Now Marcus is saying the same, resigned, as his parents were, to that not being enough for many people. He's happy to let them pull in off the road on the second of the farm's two drives, the one that runs down to the barns where Jimmy put his hand- and footprint in wet cement, happy to let them take pictures, to talk to them if he happens to be in the yard, but not keen that they should knock on his door.

The farm is unchanged since Jimmy's day, Marcus tells me, except for the addition of a new barn. It is pretty much as Jim would have known it, the fourteen-room Victorian house in the shade of a giant oak, built on a small rise overlooking the 300 acres which Marcus now rents out to other farmers. Back Creek snakes behind the house, weaving deep in the clay bed between grassy rounded banks, marking the division between garden and farmed land.

Cousin Jimmy is a bigger business than this farm for Marcus now. Everyone wants to use him, you can sell anything through the use of his face or name. Everyone from a British bank which uses his face to sell savings accounts to school-leavers, to the Gap clothing chain which uses a picture of Jimmy with the slogan 'James Dean wore khakis' to sell trousers. 'Legendary', the copy reads. 'Hollywood in the '50s. Big screen, big story. And the legendary actors, writers and rebels who found cause. All in their cotton khakis. Casual. Defiant. Khakis just like those we make for you.' While a company in Indianapolis does the donkey work, Marcus still has the final say on how his cousin's image is exploited.

'Jimmy came here in 1940,' he said, his voice a low growl, punctuating his sentences with a ruminatory ah hah, uh huh, 'and stayed for nine years. I was born in 1943 so ever since I can remember he was around.' He got up to let a dog out.

'I like it here. I guess it's our home. A lot of people say what a quiet place it is. Ah hah, uh huh. We take it for granted I guess. But you say is Jimmy's spirit still here? Ah hah, I, oh I don't know about that. I suppose in a way it is, in the whole area here of Fairmount. But we don't keep his picture hanging on the walls and things like that, everything has gone to the museum, everything we had that was his.

'Right after Jimmy's death we thought that probably after three or four years people would go on to some other celebrity or pick up on something else. Of course we knew there would be some diehard fans who would always remember him, but we never dreamed that as time went on it would be more and more fans. He died almost forty years ago and he's getting new fans all the time. It's really amazing that when someone's been gone that long . . . the momentum just keeps picking up rather than diminishing.

'It's gratifying to know that he has touched so many people's lives and influenced them, and if they bother to come here you know that he surely affected their lives in a positive way. It's nice to know he is remembered that well.'

As I prepared to leave, Marcus said again, 'Jimmy wa'n't a rebel, he was a regular guy. He liked race cars and he liked motorcycles and he liked photography and painting and sketching; he had a lot of different interests in his life and so many people relate to him because he did so many different things.'

I drove back to town via the graveyard, turning in on the white hardcore track, past the brick plinth on which the name James Dean was still picked out, but from which his bust was stolen in the Fifties. I passed a sign reading 'James Dean second drive on right top of hill' and went up a rise beneath pine trees and among the low, pink, granite headstones. A big black polished marble headstone evidently marked the grave of a rock fan whose family had confused their John Lennon with their Led Zeppelin. It had an inscription which read:

Nunn
Imagine I'm on a stairway to heaven.

There was a little Winslow family plot between a couple of pines. To Jimmy's left was the gravestone shared by Marcus and Hortense, to his right another marking his stepmother Ethel's place. The stone also had on it the name of Winton, his still-living father, and his date of birth. All it awaited was the date of death. I was told Winton was in a nursing home in Marion, too confused to talk to the people who come here because of his son. There was no grave here for

Mildred Dean, his mother, who was buried at Grant Memorial Cemetery in Marion.

Jimmy's grave was covered in open-mouthed lipstick kisses, not from one mouth but from many, in every shade of lipstick from orange to scarlet to purple. There were several bouquets of fabric flowers and on top of the pink marble grave, scarred by the chips taken out of it, lay a single black tulip. From its only slightly enervated state it could not have been here long. It would have shrivelled by the end of the day.

At the grave, a black bird with orange flashes on its shoulders, like a little construction worker in a donkey jacket, hopped between the headstones. I followed its path and caught a commotion around a white car on the next track between the graves. A girl and a woman were running towards the car. The girl was just at the driver's door, the woman fifteen, twenty paces away. The car started, revved and pulled off in a spray of white dust. The woman stopped, screeched, 'Son of a BITCH!' and doubled up, pressing her hands to the sides of her head.

I watched the white car bounce along the cemetery track, disappear behind some trees then emerge with a squeal on the road, heading south towards town. The woman was no more than fifty yards away from me so I walked towards her, feeling embarrassed and unsure of what to say. As I got close I could hear her sobbing. I asked if she was OK. She motioned me away with her left hand, pressing the heel of her right hand to her forehead and nodding. I slowed my pace but kept moving towards her.

'Was that your car?' I asked her. When she looked up I realized she was Tammi, the woman I had seen at the museum.

'Yeah,' she said uncertainly. 'My daughter . . .' the sentence died on her. I asked if she needed any help.

'I could use a cigarette,' she said, but I had to tell her I didn't have one.

'Can I give you a lift?' I pointed back past James

Dean's grave to my car on the next track. She laughed a short, hard laugh, shook her head as if in disbelief and walked past me towards it.

'I'm sorry,' she said as I pulled up level with her, 'I wasn't laughing at you.'

'Was that your daughter?' I asked.

'It sure was. Though she wishes she wa'n't.'

We got in the car and I started the engine.

'I was going back into town,' I said, 'is that OK for you?'

'Sure, we'll see Velvet just down the road. It's not the first time she's pulled this sort of stunt. Teenagers, huh?'

We drove into town. On North Main Street, across the road from the grey corner house with a sign that read James Dean Gallery, a white car was parked.

'Stop right here a second would you?' Tammi asked, so I pulled in behind the other car. 'Don't go away now,' she said, getting out and walking up to the driver's door. She aimed one smack through the open window at her daughter's face, catching her full across the cheek, then turned and walked back to me. She got in, breathed out deeply then turned to me with a tight smile. 'Can I buy you a coffee?' she asked.

As we headed on down Main I could see the white car following us in the rear-view mirror. We stopped outside Memories Diner. The white car halted a few lengths behind us, but the engine kept running. Inside was a deep room, filled with old-fashioned Formica tables at which a lot of families and elderly couples were sitting, eating the pork roast special. Trade is good, thanks to James Dean.

An overworked, cheerful waitress came up to us. There were posters of Dean and Marilyn and Elvis on the walls. We ordered coffee, then sat in silence. I was feeling a little uneasy at the situation.

'Is your daughter going to join us?' I asked.

'In time,' Tammi said. 'I'm just going to enjoy myself a little first without her messing things up. I've thought

158

of coming to Jimmy Dean's home town enough times and not done it to want to enjoy it now I'm here.'

She bought cigarettes and opened the pack immediately.

'And Fairmount is such a beautiful place,' she went on, seemingly revived by the smoke she had just inhaled. 'I've always been a fan of Jimmy Dean and I've always wanted to see where he was from. I remember my folks, when *Rebel* came out, they said I wa'n't to go see it, it was glorifying juvenile delinquents. I went to see it anyway and I just thought it was about a sweet, brave, lonely guy and I've bin in love with him ever since.

'You know, I think I married my husband because he looked like James Dean. I thought he did at the time, anyways. Now I feel like I can prove my mother wrong. You come to his home, you can see all the bad things were untrue. He wa'n't a juvenile delinquent, nothing of the kind. You can see how much they loved him to have kept all his things an' all. And to remember him and open their hearts to strangers who want to come here and remember him too . . . I just wish I coulda brought my folks here to prove to them what a sweet boy he was.

'I had his picture up in my room and magazines and all and they hated it, thought I'd gone bad. Now Velvet has his picture in her room and I encourage it. Cos I can say to her that I know exactly how she feels about that boy cos I felt just the same when I was her age. So now with Jimmy it ain't no generation-gap thing, it's the opposite.'

Except, I thought, she was in here with me and her daughter was sitting outside with a slapped face. I asked her where they had been so far and Tammi said the museum and the grave and his home. She wanted to go to the other place in town, the James Dean Gallery, but that all depended whether Velvet would start behaving. I said how about the high school and she said no she hadn't heard of that. Would I take her?

Outside Velvet was still in the white Tempo. She started the engine when we came out. Tammi approached my car then thought better of it, and turned towards her own. Velvet slid across to the passenger seat as her mother approached. 'We'll follow,' Tammi called as she opened the door. So I drove the couple of blocks between the little wooden box houses beneath the maples, pines and oaks, to the school where Adeline Nall taught Jimmy to act. There was the smell of damp even outside, of softened brick and general decay. The windows were either boarded or broken. Bob Pulley had told me that Morrissey, a big James Dean fan, had come here to make a video in 1988 and had wanted to see the Dean sights. At that time you could still go into the school and Bob had showed me a snapshot of a chalk message scrawled on a bright blue wall inside: 'Morrissey, Feb 7th 1988'. He had filmed out at the Winslow farm, riding on a tractor. I mentioned all this and saw the look of permanent disdain on Velvet's face be replaced by one of wide-eyed interest.

Then we went to the James Dean Gallery, back up Main Street. I sat on the porch talking to the guy who runs it while Velvet and Tammi joined the handful of others walking round the exhibitions of movie artefacts, and vast collection of anything and everything that had Dean's picture on it.

David Loehr, a nervous New Yorker, started this collection nineteen years ago, having seen the movies back to back at a festival on a big screen. He was captivated by Dean's look, the way he moved and his unquantifiable magnetism. Fourteen years ago Loehr was travelling from California to New York and decided to go via Fairmount. He went out to the farm. Five years ago, after many other visits, he found this house was vacant and decided to bring himself and his collection here.

'I don't know what it is about Dean that attracts me,' he said. 'It's more of a feeling than anything else, it's just something: charisma. A lot of it is in his looks,

160

the way that he moved, he was one of a kind. He was the first one to be like that, the first American teenager. Before that, teenagers didn't really have an identity. He was before rock and roll and he inspired rock and roll. He just inspires every generation. He has inspired Elvis and the Beatles, now I find out the lead singer of Pearl Jam is a big James Dean fan, and Morrissey. Now we get a lot of Morrissey fans here who aren't necessarily Jimmy Dean fans, but they come to see where Morrissey made his video.

'When I first came to Fairmount the museum was in a different building and just had a tiny Dean display upstairs, and there wasn't much to see here. But I went out to the farm. Aunt Hortense was still living then. I was with a friend and we went and knocked on the door.

'It happened to be Mothers' Day. Hortense was gracious, she welcomed us in and we sat and talked with her for a little while. And after a while I asked if I could see Jimmy's room and she said "Why does everybody always want to see his room?" But she said sure, asked me if I'd care to vacuum her upstairs for her and she got about halfway up the stairs and she started to cry. And I thought uh uh, and then I realized it was Mothers' Day and it was bringing things back, memories I guess. She didn't bawl, she just started getting teary-eyed.

'The room was exactly as he had left it. His things were still on the desk and his bed was there and his drawings were still on the wall and his books were on the shelf. It did feel strange, yeah, and his bongos were sitting there and his cowboy boots.

'I'm sure there must have been a time when the family wished it would just be over with because they could never forget the fact that Jimmy was dead. Somebody dies who is close to you, there comes a time you begin to forget about it, but when it is like with Jimmy and his fans, every day a constant reminder, it's got to get hard to take at times.'

David took me inside to show me around. He had everything from clothing worn by Dean in his films to a plastic thimble with his picture on it. He showed me one of the things he was proudest of: a short length of white-painted garden fence. Not just any bit of garden fence, but the fence from the Los Angeles location used for the back gate to James Dean's parents' house. 'They were getting ready to throw this out, they were putting up a block wall. I tried to talk to them but the lady wouldn't open the door. She said "You can take that old wood" so I threw it in the car and shipped it back here. It's a bit of Hollywood history, the kind of thing that makes you think you are doing the right thing, the timing and all.'

We were back sitting on the porch when Tammi and Velvet came out. David talked to Tammi while Velvet stared at him. Tammi was saying how much Velvet loved it here, how much she loved James Dean, how she had put a flower on his grave, a black tulip, how she was so romantic in a doomed kind of way.

David looked at Velvet and asked her which was her favourite movie.

'Oh,' she said, 'I haven't seen any of his movies, I just like his looks.' Then she changed the subject, suddenly saying to David, 'Do you know you look just like Morrissey?' She was right, he did.

'Uh huh, I've heard that,' said David uncomfortably, and turned back to Tammi. But Velvet kept on staring at him as if he really was Morrissey and really was worth looking at, much more interesting than some long-dead actor. I imagined her in twenty years, returning to Fairmount to show *her* daughter not the Dean sights but the ruined high school where Morrissey chalked his name, the tractor Morrissey sat on, and to show her the guy who looks just like him.

It was David who told me about Adeline, taking me back into the gallery after Tammi and Velvet had left, and calling her to see if she could see me. I headed north to find her, and as I drove I reflected on the Dean appeal, on the story of an orphan who died young.

As with Marilyn Monroe and Elvis Presley, it seemed to me, if you wanted to get to the emotional essence of his continuing attraction you had to strip away the stardom and the talent because they, while essentials to fame, somehow obscure the true nature of his appeal.

To get to that, you need to see him not as a great actor, not a role model, not the first teenager, but simply as a universal orphan figure who died young and whom we can all mourn as members of a kind of universal family.

And he was a victim, like Marilyn and Elvis. A victim twice over – once when his mother died, again when Turnupseed killed him.

The people who come to Fairmount to remember James Dean are reacting to this boy/man less as a movie star, more as if he had been a brother, a son, a lover or whatever the appropriate relationship is to them personally. And they come into a welcoming small-town community which sees him in exactly those ways, not as an international star but as Jim Dean, the popular, regular guy, good at sports, who made it big in the city but who never forgot his roots and his love of his home town and its people.

Add to that the fact that he died young, that in death he has achieved immortality, is frozen permanently at his prime through the life-giving elixir of the movies, and you have a perfect combination.

Anyone can enter into Dean's life because of the welcome they will get in his home town, from his friends and family. The appeal in coming here is that you step for a day or two into a real-life soap opera. And I loved it. I loved every little memento in the museum, every little detail that Jimmy's old friends and family could give me about him.

Most people don't live in small towns where everybody knows everybody else, where everyone looks out for each other, but they still hold that kind of life up as something of an ideal. The American ideal of the small town lives on in Fairmount thanks to James Dean, whose popularity has stopped the businesses on Main Street from going broke, who now sustains the town that made him.

Here, using your interest in James Dean as the key, you can open up small-town life, step in and live it a little, going to Bob Pulley's house to look through his yearbooks, talking to Marky out on the farm, visiting Adeline the former high-school teacher.

I, like thousands of others, had turned up on Fairmount's doorstep saying, 'Hi, I'm a friend of Jim's,' and been greeted with the words, 'Anyone who is a friend of Jimmy's is a friend of ours. Come on in.'

CHAPTER NINE

Another Angel?

RIVER PHOENIX,
LOS ANGELES, 31 OCTOBER

Fairmount had reintroduced me to small town America, and reminded me how wonderful it could be, and what a joy it was coasting on back roads through the American countryside. My next destination was another small town, Plainfield, nearly 600 miles away. In two weeks' time, which was when I needed to be there, the northern landscape of Wisconsin would be wintry.

As I was in no hurry I devised a lazy, roundabout route for myself, taking back roads and stopping at run-down out-of-town motels, where if the room had a pink plastic flyswat in a drawer it counted as a luxury apartment. I loped west into Illinois and picked up a good old-fashioned two-lane road – Highway 51 – which set up echoes in my memory of a song on Bob Dylan's first album called 'Highway 51 Blues'. My recollection was a little hazy, but I recall dear old Bob was groaning away about it being the road that went past his baby's door. What I do remember relatively clearly is the line about the road running from Wisconsin way down to no-man's-land.

As I drove I pursued my hobby of collecting the more inane mottos I saw on roadside signs. Outside a high school I read 'Success comes in cans. Failure comes in can'ts.' Another advised 'Feel joy in what you give, not in what you get.' On a truck I saw 'Have courage to let go of the things not worth sticking to.' Like the road, perhaps? Finally, I noticed that some warped, cynical bastard had put out one reading 'This sign is blank.'

I travelled through a vast, flat, empty land, as Bob Dylan had told me I would. I switched on the radio and found I had tuned straight into Radio Garrison Keillor. 'It was a quiet night in Mount Vernon, according to police,' intoned the newsreader. 'A teen fell asleep at the wheel and crashed, but his five passengers were not hurt. There were two reports of theft. Jewels disappeared from a house, and juveniles were questioned. A wallet was taken at the High School while its owner played basketball.'

As the radio burbled quietly in the background the landscape fell into a soothing pattern. The farms were little islands of habitation in the frozen expanse, each with a silver cylindrical grain store and a house with a green felt roof and surrounded by trees. Green and silver and white were the only colours. The farms, a mile or so apart, were strung together by power lines carried on brown pylons crafted to resemble trees. Every ten or fifteen miles there was a little town like Assumption, with a John Deere showroom selling green combine harvesters and tractors on one side of the road, and a Case showroom offering similar machines in red on the other.

As I moved into Wisconsin the land became covered with conifer plantations, and the farm buildings wore an ochre and green uniform instead of green and white. The weather was appalling up here, heavy rain if I was lucky, snow if I was not.

I was driving, lulled by the rain, the swish of the windscreen wipers and the murmuring radio, when suddenly an announcer mentioned something about the death of the new James Dean and I thought hold on a minute.

An actor called River Phoenix was dead, at the age of twenty-three. He had expired in a Sunset Strip nightclub on, would you believe it, Hallowe'en.

166

So, like the death-site tourist I had become, I changed my itinerary and got myself down to Chicago and onto the first flight to Los Angeles. Sure enough there were flowers on the pavement on Sunset Boulevard when I arrived, the day after the death. I found myself sniffing the air with my practised nose as I stood outside the club called the Viper Room where, thirty-six hours before, River Phoenix had died. Could I scent a cult in the making?

It was on this patch of pavement beneath the black awning that, at 1 a.m. on 31 October, River went into drug-induced seizures and died. Beside a parking meter, the shrine was already in place. Like the others I had seen, there were the candles, the flowers and the graffiti. 'River was real and always stood for truth' I read. 'Without even touching me, you invaded my soul, and I miss you.' There were plenty more. Rivers flowed into seas. Phoenixes rose from ashes.

This twenty-three-year-old actor had died thirty-eight years, one month and one day after Dean, but to me, the memory of the Dean death drive still fresh in my mind, it seemed like just a month and a day.

Had a new myth been created on this patch of grubby pavement? Had I caught River Phoenix in the act of stepping up there alongside Jimmy and Marilyn and Elvis? I wasn't the only one wondering.

I bought up all the newspapers and magazines which had a mention of him and found many other people were wondering too. It all struck me as self-conscious in the extreme. When James Dean died no-one asked if he would live for ever. Nor Marilyn, nor Elvis. But, because they pulled off that particular neat little trick, we all seemed to expect that others would, too. Dead for only a matter of hours, River Phoenix seemed to have been promoted automatically to the ranks of the forever young. We would see.

It was rather eerie, halfway through my tour of the death sites of established icons, to find another star drop dead at my feet. It was like that nasty thrill you feel when television suddenly goes live to the scene of a disaster and you get caught up with all the other front-row rubberneckers.

The death tourists came flocking. The Viper Room was busier than ever. But the stars – Johnny Depp, a co-owner, and River's girlfriend Samantha Mathis and younger brother Leaf, who were with him when he died – now stayed well away. There were no celebs when I called in, no drugs in the men's room as the tabloids crowed was the case when River OD'd. There were just Australian tourists and big-haired girls from the suburbs, all stumbling around in the gloom like me, pretending that we had all been here a zillion times before on the nights when River would get up with his guitar and jam with the band.

River? I loved that guy!

I did my best to go on a River death tour, but the sites were few. River never had a home in Los Angeles, but stayed in the St James's club, a 1930s apartment block turned hotel where the security guards made sure grieving fans remained outside its grand white walls.

I looked for relics, too, finding only one. But for ghoulishness it took the prize salami. I discovered that a tape existed of the conversation Leaf Phoenix had with the ambulance service when he dialled 911 after River's seizure. I found out that if you went to the ambulance headquarters in East L.A. they would usher you into an office in which a ghetto-blaster sat on top of a filing cabinet. They gave me a tape to snap into the machine and on it I heard Leaf shouting so loudly that the tape distorted, in a mix of fear and rage.

They left me to listen in private. I heard Leaf veering between a weepy, panicked rage and a sort of strung-out politeness as he asked, begged and demanded that they do something to help his brother. Just before the tape clicked off he apologized to the ambulance despatcher for having been so rude.

Perhaps one can see Phoenix as a Dean for the Nineties.

There were those who had compared him with Dean from the time of the release of his 1986 film *Stand By Me*, about a bunch of kids trekking off cross-country to find the body of a murdered friend. He had the chiselled cheek-bones, intense stare and gawky adolescent slouch. On screen he had the gravity, sensitivity, fragility, and vulnerability that Dean revealed.

Dean's *Rebel Without a Cause* and Phoenix's *My Own Private Idaho* can certainly both be seen as dealing with the problems of teenagers growing up in the 1950s and 1990s respectively. *Rebel* deals with the 1950s problems of affluence, delinquency and the decline of moral standards, *Idaho* with the 1990s scourges of poverty, broken homes, drugs and exploitation. In both, the heroes are appealing because of their vulnerability. They are archetypal troubled young men coming of age.

With Phoenix, the key question was: would he move from being a reasonably successful actor to a cultural icon? Only time would tell, but it was clear he had a number of the credentials.

I was to ponder over River Phoenix for the rest of my journey, and for the months afterwards, awaiting the first anniversary of his death. That anniversary would show whether a cult was in the making or not.

Meanwhile, I drove up from the smoggy hollow of Hollywood, and wound the car up the tree-covered road to Griffith Park, east of the Hollywood sign. In the comparatively clean air where the Griffith Observatory stands and where several key scenes of *Rebel Without a Cause* were shot, I leant on the railing close to the plinth on which a black bust of James Dean rests, looked down on Sunset Strip and west towards Hollywood, and thought some more about River.

Phoenix's life story certainly had a contemporary ring to it, and sufficient mystery and romance for interest in him to grow after his death. If we could still create Strange Angels – which I doubted – surely he would become one.

River was born in a log cabin in Oregon to a couple of roving hippies and named after the river of life in Herman Hesse's *Siddhartha*. The parents, John and Arlyn, became missionaries for the controversial Children of God in Venezuela, but left the church when they grew disillusioned with the lavish lifestyle of its leader, David Berg, and his policy of trying to attract rich converts through sex.

The family moved to Florida, and decided on a totally new course of life. The five children – River, Leaf, Rainbow, Liberty and Summer – would become actors and the parents would be their managers. They changed their name to Phoenix as a symbol of their rebirth, keeping their former name a secret. They were vegan, and shunned modern medicine, leading a true alternative lifestyle. At nine, River was winning talent shows, and at ten he had moved with his mother to Hollywood, where he did commercials. But he objected to selling products he knew nothing about. Later he said, 'I felt that the constant lying, the smiling on cue and the product-naming was going to drive me crazy.'

He made *Stand By Me*, his first big hit, in 1985 when he was fifteen and was hailed as a natural, instinctive actor. Never having been to school, it was said, meant that he did not think himself into a role but felt his way in.

By 1988 four films had been released, River was on his way to making $1m a picture, and was feeling the temptations of fame. Girls camped around his hotel. Although he always expressed himself vehemently anti-drug, he seems to have started experimenting with heroin during the filming of *My Own Private Idaho*, perhaps to try and get into the little-rent-boy-lost character he played.

In '88 the family moved back to Florida, settling on twenty acres in Gainsville, having decided that

Hollywood was too corrupting a place for them to be exposed to full-time.

In interviews, River talked earnestly about animals and ecology. He espoused the causes of youth, saying in one magazine interview: 'I feel I intuitively come to the defence of the Earth's rights. I'm against the nuclear arms race and apartheid in South Africa and cruelty to animals, which means I'm a vegetarian. Diet is a good place to start making a change because it's something I can do, I can't change the regime in South Africa or teach Palestinians how to live with Israelis, but I can start with me.'

He was beautiful and vulnerable, sensitive and alienated, thinking and confused. To his young fans he seemed just like them: non-materialistic, scruffy, idealistic, committed to all the right causes and concerns. He talked of using his money to buy tracts of Brazilian rain forest, or to build homeless shelters in the States.

There was some suggestion, when the Los Angeles coroner's report revealed that River died of a deadly cocktail of drugs – lethal amounts of cocaine and morphine with traces of heroin, marijuana and valium – that there would be a strong reaction against him, that the double life he had led would destroy his reputation. That seemed doubtful. River once said, 'I lie all the time. One, it gives me some variety and secondly they will change the truth anyhow, so I may as well say what I like.'

Wouldn't his fans relate to that? And even more so when he said, 'I am confused. I go back and forth about success and wealth and want to take the Devil's bribe and use it for God.'

As I left Hollywood for the last time, headed first back on my broken journey to Wisconsin, and later down south to Dallas for the thirtieth anniversary of the assassination of John F. Kennedy, I kept an eye on the Phoenix cult.

The reaction to Phoenix's death from fans was

powerful. Magazines got hundreds of letters, in which River was described as one of the geniuses of our time. There was a rush for his videos from rental stores, and numerous articles from – principally – young women trying to express, and explain to themselves, the strength of their feelings at his death. Jessica Berens in the *Daily Telegraph* was typical: 'It made me want to go to a funeral, build a shrine, put on a black armband. He was not a personal friend so why the sense of loss? Surely we have grown out of the unreal relationships that enervate our teenage years – the fantasy friendship with the poster on the wall.'

In the weeks after Phoenix's death I corresponded with fans in Europe, America and Japan, and found that their reactions were uniform. Their immediate responses were, one, they found it hard to believe, two, they were stung by a sense of personal loss.

From the Japanese fan club, Mizuho Nakanishi said that she was not sad, did not cry because the fact of River's death had not hit her yet. 'I feel as if I am reading his new movie's story.'

A London schoolgirl called Sabrina Chetrian wrote: 'I didn't really know about all the films he did . . . I didn't really fancy him or anything. But hearing he'd died I felt really shocked. It wasn't someone I really knew or noticed. But he was part of our generation. I felt closer to the thought of death. He was young, closer to our age and I thought that if he could be here one minute and gone the next, it was scary. So could we.'

Frequently it was to the perceived personal strengths of River Phoenix that the fans referred. Josephine Teale, a sixteen-year-old, was clearly attracted to what she believed to be the essence of Phoenix as a person (as I had seen with the followers of Marilyn, Dean and Elvis), when she wrote: 'He was a very deep and caring person, he was sensitive and intelligent and very loving, he was also very close to his family.' She sought an explanation for his death: 'Maybe River unconsciously wanted to die. Who would ever take a quantity of drugs so lethal that it would instantly kill them unless they wanted to die?'

There were those who were angry with Phoenix because he died in the way he did. Kelly Young said, 'I feel angry and betrayed by him . . . He had always preached about so many things I agreed with and believed in, like vegetarianism, "saving the world" and against drug abuse. He has such a vast following, he could have made so many see the light, he could have done so much good in the world . . . he had practically condemned the Hollywood life, the parties and falseness that came with it and almost vowed he would never become a part of it. He knew better than most, he had seen from his extraordinary life the perils of drug-taking, and he allowed himself to be sucked into the lifestyle he had promoted as wrong. He allowed his life to be wasted, he threw it away. I feel . . . as if he lied to us, and most of all I feel angry with him for letting it happen.' Here was the last person, she said, who she would have expected to die in this way.

At English public schools, including Benenden, Roedean and Cheltenham Ladies' College, there were reports of weeping younger girls being comforted by their elders, of makeshift shrines, special prayers and plans to screen the films. When I followed them up I got sniffy responses which seemed only to confirm the strength of feeling I had first heard about.

Cheltenham's vice-principal, Mary Prince, said, 'There were no tears shed nor makeshift shrines erected for River Phoenix . . . while the death of this young actor was unexpected and quite a shock, the girls at the Ladies' College have kept the situation in perspective, and felt that the recent spate of killings in Northern Ireland, for example, is a far greater cause for concern.'

I bet they did, when encouraged to think rationally about it. But three weeks on, whom did they remember, the terrorists' victims, or River Phoenix? I'll gamble on it being the latter.

There were similarities in all this to the death of Dean. The initial reaction then was one of disbelief. Fans wanted to keep him alive, and flocked to fan clubs to try and do so. But there were differences as well, differences of degree which, as the months passed, were clearly substantial. The reaction to Dean grew and grew. Four months after his death, in January '56, 3,000 letters were received by Warner Brothers, Dean's film company. By July the number was 7,000 a month, and at the time of the first anniversary 50,000 had been received, more than for any living star.

At Phoenix's Japanese and American fan clubs – no others had been formed by October 1994 – the stream of letters, numbering several hundred a month shortly after the death, dropped off to a trickle by the time of the first anniversary. The studio-star system which Dean was a part of no longer existed when River died, so there was not the same focus for fans. I talked to his manager Tris Burton who said, 'We haven't had that kind of response and we don't want it. I prefer not to talk about him. We are still in mourning.'

With Dean there was a scramble for souvenirs, and tiny pieces of his car were sold, as well as fake locks of hair and a wide range of trinkets bearing his picture. On Hollywood Boulevard, my spies told me, there was no sign of River joining Marilyn, Jimmy and Elvis on the T-shirts, mugs and posters. No official posters were issued on either side of the Atlantic. At the Vintage Magazine Company, a hip London poster shop, they had a bootleg poster taken from the publicity shot for *My Own Private Idaho* which, at the time of the anniversary, was selling 100 copies a week. This was about the same as for James Dean pictures, but less than their bestseller – for the film *Reservoir Dogs* – at 150 a week.

One way fans could show their interest – which Dean fans did not have at the time of his death – was by the purchase of video versions of Phoenix's films. But take the sales of *Stand By Me*, for example, and you see no rise after his death. UK sales figures were 24,000 in 1991, 13,000 in 1992, 8,000 in 1993 (the year he died) and 2,000 in 1994.

As 31 October came round again it was clear that, unlike Dean, Phoenix did not become a bigger star after his death. There was no sign that he would become a James Dean, despite the fact that he seemed to share so many of his qualities and to mirror so much of his appeal.

I can see only one conclusion to draw from this. It is that we simply don't make Strange Angels any more. We want our icons to come from the past, not the present. We want them to embody all the rosy-tinted appeal of a lost time of perceived hope and happiness. Today's stars are so tainted, either during their lives or – in Phoenix's case – shortly after it, that they do not have the power to sustain our interest, let alone our adulation.

CHAPTER TEN

The Marsh Angel

ED GEIN, PLAINFIELD,
WISCONSIN, 16 NOVEMBER

It was dark, and the rain was heavy when I got to Plainfield. So I could hear the screaming but could not see where it came from. It sounded like a group of children shrieking in animal terror, somewhere off across the parking lot, away from the log cabin of the truckstop.

In my headlights, reduced to a weak yellow glow by the powering rain, I could see the shadowy forms of a line of parked-up trucks. I drove towards them, my wipers thrashing, window open to get a bearing on the sound. Rain drenched my left shoulder and the side of my face. The screaming was coming from the end of the line of trucks. It was coming from the long silver trailer of the end truck. Not until I was alongside the vehicle did I realize what was making the noise. The lorry was loaded with pigs, packed with pigs, pigs on three levels screaming and clattering on their metal floors, panicking in the storm, biting into each other's flesh. And the rain came splattering down like blood in the dark.

At the time, exhausted from my race to Los Angeles and back, and my long, late-night drive north from Chicago, it seemed like a waking nightmare in a nightmare of a place. But, next morning, frozen Plainfield was bathed in a brilliant winter's sun and the episode had lost its power to chill. I even wondered whether it had happened.

It was easy to believe, as well, that the other, far greater horror, had never happened. That no human blood was ever wilfully spilled in Plainfield, Wisconsin, no graves robbed, no trophies cut from bodies. That no grotesque female face masks were crafted from dead tissue, no breasts and vaginas severed, tanned and worn by a man. It was easy to believe that the man whom nobody will talk about never existed. But if that were so, Robert Bloch could not have written *Psycho*, and Thomas Harris would not have written *The Silence of the Lambs*.

Such a peaceful, ordinary little town.

I could stand on the balcony of the Johnson Inn and look clean through Plainfield. I could see clear down North Street, past the bowling alley with its Fresh Pizza sign, past the Shell station and the bar with its pine shingles, past the empty stores, the shut-down K and S bar and grill, past the intersection with wide, stunted Main Street where City Hall is situated above a garage housing two snowploughs. I could see past Fran's Coffee Cup and as far as Charlie's hardware store.

You would think that the Johnson Inn might hold some clues to the terrible story of Plainfield, for the Johnsons have made their bed-and-breakfast lodge a self-consciously historic place. Nancy and Burrell have named the rooms after prominent Plainfield families. There is the Vroman dining-room, named after the first potato-farming family in Plainfield; the Bowen kitchen, after Nancy's cookery teacher; the Bound library, after Thelma Bound, a community librarian; the Spear bathroom, after Plainfield's first plumber, and the wicker and lace Rothermel Room, named after Florence Rothermel, a local schoolteacher.

But there was no room named Worden, and none named Gein. Yet the horror had touched here too, as I would find out later, touched Burrell and Nancy Johnson as it had touched everyone else in Plainfield. I found myself listing the things in the house, in echo

177

and contrast to another list I had read, and Robert Bloch had read, and Thomas Harris.

The list I made in the Johnson Inn was of the things that made it homely, human, welcoming. There were the parlour things: a fireplace with mahogany pillars running up through the mantel and forming an arch over the mirror, a clock with a glass front revealing the pendulum, a corner cabinet filled with china, two brass candlesticks holding purple candles, a basket of fabric flowers, a bird in a wicker cage, three kinds of artificial logs in three baskets, a long floral sofa and two pink armchairs, a side table with a lamp, a standard lamp, a little low piano like a writing desk, a cabinet full of toy red tractors, and a tape deck playing New Age music. In my bedroom there were a patchwork quilt in greens with pink, repeating the colours on the walls, a doll mouse in a cap, a salmon pink dress and a pinafore, with a smaller mouse in the pocket of the pinafore. A silver plate holding four chocolates, two wrapped in silver paper, one in green and one in pink. And a note reading 'A kiss to dream on. Goodnight.'

The list in the Gein house was altogether different. It went like this: two shin-bones, a pair of human lips on a string, a cup full of human noses on the kitchen table, a purse with a handle made of skin and human skin bracelets, four cane-seated chairs, the cane replaced with woven human skin, ten skulls, a human-skin tom-tom on a quart can, a bowl made from half a skull, skins of four women's faces, rouged, made up and pinned to the wall at eye level, five other faces in plastic bags, ten female heads hacked off at the eyebrows, a rolled-up pair of leggings and a skin vest including mammaries.

In the smokehouse next door to the summer kitchen a human heart, Bernice Worden's heart, floated in a pan of water on the stove. The freezer compartment of the fridge was stocked with wrapped human organs. And in the middle of the room was Bernice Worden's nude, headless body dangling by the heels, disembowelled like a butchered deer.

You will probably never have heard of Ed Gein and Bernice Worden. I hadn't either until I stumbled upon their story. And then I discovered that, though he was an anonymous figure, Ed Gein had had an impact on the public imagination that could be placed alongside that of James Dean and Marilyn Monroe. I'm not suggesting that if his name were known he would become a cult figure of the magnitude of either of them, or of Elvis. He certainly would not become an idol, a hero or a role model to anybody but the terribly sick. In Ed Gein I had stumbled upon a person who had nevertheless had a significant impact on many millions of people – but this time without them knowing anything about him. And he interested me because, while the other Strange Angels I was writing about were very public figures, and their impact on our imaginations were there for everyone to see, Gein was a totally private figure, and *his* impact on our imaginations went unrecognized.

Gein was a character so bizarre, responsible for crimes so appalling, so shocking in their inhumanity, that they had been the basis for two major works of fiction, and two hugely popular films, created thirty years apart. It intrigued me that, with all the horrors that the human imagination could dream up, *Psycho* and *The Silence of the Lambs* both had their genesis in fact – the same fact. What was also chilling, being in Plainfield and hearing the grisly details of the Ed Gein story, was that neither film could match the true story for horrors. *The Silence of the Lambs* was terrifying enough, but Ed Gein did worse – far worse – than anything Hannibal – the cannibal – Lecter and Jame Gumb (a.k.a. Buffalo Bill) ever achieved.

And whereas a place such as Fairmount was delighted to recall its links with James Dean, and Jonesboro with Scarlett O'Hara, Plainfield very much wanted to forget about Ed Gein.

I walked through town to get the feel of the place. I was drawn to the hardware store, which smelt of galvanized cans and fertilizer. I had arrived in Plainfield in early November, just a few days before the anniversary, on 16 November, of the day on which, in 1957, Ed Gein walked into this store. In those days it bore Bernice's surname – Worden – but was now called Charlie's. Gein shot Bernice dead with a rifle from her own display, slit her throat and carried her away. That was the first day of the deer-hunting season. Sixty-eight deer were registered in the area on the first day of the 1957 season. One kill was not registered, though the carcass was later found strung up in Ed Gein's shed.

He was only suspected of the crime by chance. Bernice's son Frank remembered Gein saying he might pop into the store on Saturday to buy antifreeze, and the last purchase marked in the store's ledger, in his mother's handwriting, was for a half-gallon of this. Frank, who was a deputy sheriff, had had his suspicions of the simple, shambling, fifty-one-year-old bachelor since Mary Hogan, the owner of a tavern in a hamlet a few miles north of Plainfield, had disappeared in December 1954. A pool of blood was found on the floor, and a trail leading, presumably, to where a vehicle had stood. He found a similar pool of blood, and a gory trail, in his mother's shop.

When the law officers visited Gein's remote, ram-shackle farm seven miles south of town, Gein was away from home. The farm had no electricity but, in the light of their torches, they uncovered a collection of horrors that were unique in their grotesqueness. Although Gein was only ever tried for one murder, it was clear from what they found that they had a serial killer, an habitual grave-robber and – probably – a cannibal on their hands.

The first thing they saw when they pushed in the door of a woodshed was the nude headless body of Bernice Worden hanging from the rafters by her ankles. They moved on, and found a mask created from Mary Hogan's face behind the kitchen door, then Mrs Worden's heart on the stove. Later, Gein insisted he was not going to eat it, but burn it. In the living-room was a medical textbook, with the pages on the human head and female reproductive organs well-thumbed. Most of the rooms were filthy, full of discarded food tins and old newspapers, but two were totally different. Gein had nailed shut the living-room and bedroom that were used by his mother, and they were preserved just as she had left them. This contrast was later seen to hint at a mother-fixation, and to a possible incestuous relationship.

The search went on all night, and it was not until 4.30 a.m. that they found Bernice Worden's head hidden in a bag wedged between two old mattresses. A nail had been inserted in each ear-socket and string passed between them so the head could be hung up like a trophy.

The police officers had uncovered the remains of many victims. Gein admitted that he had dug up nine or ten bodies between 1950 and 1954 from three local cemeteries, including the one at Plainfield where his mother, father and brother were buried. He may have robbed as many as forty graves. He said he would take the face of the freshly-buried body and place it over his own face, and take the vagina and place it over his penis. He would also dress up in the hair and breasts of his victims and prance around his farm on moonlit nights. Several of the women he dug up, he said, had been chosen because of their resemblance to his mother.

Some of the findings at the farm led to the suspicion that Gein had murdered other women. They found the vulvas of two girls aged about fifteen; as there were no girls aged between twelve and eighteen in the local cemeteries, there was a strong suspicion that Gein had had a hand in the disappearance of two teen-agers, Evelyn Hartley from La Crosse and Jane Weckler from Jefferson. Two men from Chicago whom Gein had offered to take hunting also disappeared. The jacket of one of them, and his dog, were found in the woods near Gein's home. Perhaps their car had been sunk in the swamps in the woods, as happens to Norman Bates's first victim in *Psycho*.

Gein was also suspected of killing his brother, Henry, whose body was found on a pile of undergrowth that he and Gein had been burning in the woods on their farm in 1944.

And yet, close to the thirty-sixth anniversary of Bernice Worden's murder, Plainfield was such a bright and cheerful place that it was hard to imagine these things happening here. The temperature was well below freezing, but everything was sparkling in the sunshine. And the people were friendly, trusting souls. Until you mentioned Ed Gein.

I went into Fran's Coffee Cup, on the corner of North Street and Main opposite the hardware store. It was a long, deep, gloomy room. At the front were a jukebox and three video games, unplugged, a pool table with a notice saying that if you knocked a ball to the floor you had to put 50c in the jukebox, some racks of second-hand clothes which seemed to have overflowed from the thrift store next door, an ancient cash register, and two hefty old Kelvinator ice-cream cabinets. A long bar with plastic stools ran the length of the room, which was carpeted with a rucked old mustard affair that made it smell like a musty, dusty Scout hut.

There were two women working, younger and older. The older sat at the junk-shop end of the room, the other took my order. I sat at the bar sipping my coffee, looking at a mix of things on the shelf behind the counter, a tin of extra-large green boiled peas beside a pack of disposable lighters, jars of tootsie rolls, root-beer barrels and other one-cent candies, a wooden fretwork sign saying Fran, and a notice headed:

Answers $1.
To a question that requires thought $2.
Correct answers $4.
Dumb looks are still free.

I asked the waitress if I could have an answer to a $2 question and separated the bills from my change, pushing them towards her. She looked from them to me, her good nature freezing. 'Where can I find Ed Gein's house?' I asked. She gave me a dumb look. No charge so far. Two women gossiping at a table behind me fell silent. I felt their disapproval beamed at my back.

'We don't like to talk about such things here,' she said to me. 'In fact we are offended that people like you come here and want to drag up something that happened over thirty-five years ago.' Nancy Johnson at the inn reacted similarly when I asked her. They did not like the fact that Ed Gein was the only reason why Plainfield was remarkable. And in this house it was particularly unfortunate that I should mention the man, because Bernice Worden had been Burrell's aunt.

This was the first time during my travels that people had been reluctant to talk about a person I was interested in. Such reticence seemed curiously un-American. I had half expected Ed Gein T-shirts in the stores and a sign saying Welcome to Plainfield, home of *Psycho*. Whatever locals may hope, Ed Gein is not going to go away.

At the time of the killings it was hard to discover the details of what Gein had done. The local papers found his acts unspeakable and his story largely unprintable. Robert Bloch was living forty miles from Plainfield, in a small town called Weyauwega, at the time of the Worden murder and Gein's swift arrest.

'I just learned the bare bones from the local paper,' he told me. 'Even in its sanitized form this was very shocking in 1957. The idea that in Middle America, in a squeaky-clean small town, there could be a serial killer and grave-robber was appalling. It was a mystery, too. Everybody in a small town knows everybody else's business. It baffled me how he could have gotten away with it for so long. I thought, there is a story here, and I started writing *Psycho*. Nothing was said about Gein. So I had to invent the real life, the mind in which such crimes could be conceived.'

He invented a man called Norman Bates, a mother-fixated, transvestite mass murderer, who killed during memory lapses in which his mother's personality took over. Because grave-robbing was beyond the pale for mainstream fiction at the time, Bloch gave Bates a motel to enable his character's easy access to strangers. Bloch's great master-stroke was inventing the shower murder scene. That owed nothing to Gein, but – years later when he learned the details of the case – Bloch found that a great deal else that he had imagined mirrored reality.

'I was shocked by the similarities with what I had invented, that I had been able to invent a person and a course of action that so closely mirrored the real-life activities of Ed Gein. Gein was not a transvestite – he was worse, he actually dressed up in women's bodies. He was mother-fixated and also given to amnesiac fugues so that he did not recall the details of his activities. I found it very disturbing that I had it in me to imagine what Ed Gein had actually done.'

When Thomas Harris came to write *The Silence of the Lambs*, his character Jame Gumb (Buffalo Bill), who murders and flays women because he is making a woman's skin for himself to wear, is closer to Gein than Bates was.

Harris was briefed on the details of the Gein case by Robert K. Ressler of the FBI Behavioral Science Unit, the activities of which are the focus of the book and film. Ressler also introduced him to the FBI agent who became the model for his heroine, Clarice Starling.

Starling tries to gain vital clues in the hunt for Buffalo Bill by talking to the deranged cannibalistic killer Dr Hannibal Lecter. Like Gein, Jame Gumb kills women, peels their skins off, and crafts them into a garment which he can wear, a woman's body that he can get inside. Like Gein, like Norman Bates, he is obsessed with his dead mother. Perhaps he wanted to become his mother, as Gein may also have wished.

The silence in Plainfield about Gein was deafening. In the week I spent there, I tried all sorts of tacks to get people to talk about him. I went to the local newspaper offices in a little town called Wautoma, beside a restaurant which displayed a sign proclaiming proudly

New Owner
Swedish Meatballs

Hey Swedish, how ya doin'? Wautoma styles itself The Christmas Tree Capital of the World and its parking meters cost just one cent for twelve minutes. I poured over back issues of the *Waushara Argus*, which gave scant details of the Gein case, mentioned vaguely that 'an avalanche of physical evidence has been recovered which will take weeks and possibly months to completely evaluate and process'. The reporters, and the women selling classified ads, were as tight-lipped as their file copies.

I talked to bar-room bores including a guy who tried to tempt me to sample a turkey gizzard from the oversize pickle jar that sat beneath the hunting notices on the other side of the bar. He was swilling them down with his Bud. I asked about Gein, he told me about the dog slumbering beside his stool. 'This dog won't bite,' he complained as he struggled to hook a piece of turkey gizzard from a molar.

'Oh really?'

'Yep. I've tried training him up, but it's just no good.'

'Is it a problem?'

'Yep. Cos I got some people needs biting.'

I think he meant me.

In another bar, a guy called Rich wearing an electric-blue bomber jacket said he knew where the Gein place was, and offered to take me there. I felt like I was doing him a favour taking him out of the bar because Rich, a ratty little character with straw-like blond hair looking like it had been stuck on inexpertly with superglue, was trying to chat up the girlfriend of a very meaty-looking guy in a cowboy hat every time he went off to play the video driving game.

We got in my car and he directed me east. It was only sitting next to him in the car that I realized how drunk he was. At the edge of town he took me south, then east again, then south, then on a road that weaved so much I lost all sense of direction. It started to snow and became dark: I had to put my headlights on. I began to worry. Finally he said woah woah. We stopped, at a break in the trees which opened onto a stretch of rising ground with a shadowy house at the top of the rise. 'There she is,' said Rich.

The house was a clearly abandoned, green-painted, two-storey clapboard affair built sideways onto the road. I recalled the picture of Gein's house I had seen in the newspaper. This was not it, and I told Rich so. 'Hey,' he said, 'who is supposed to know? You or me?'

Robert Bloch has a theory about why people in Plainfield are so reluctant to talk about Gein, even thirty-six years after the murder. It is that there remains a sense of collective guilt in the community. That, because Gein was among them for so long, prattling about sex changes and murderers who made big mistakes, joking about being involved in the disappearances of women and bragging about his collection of shrunken heads, and no-one thought to do anything about it, they are all implicated. While they kept quiet about his extreme strangeness he was robbing up to forty fresh graves. How could no-one have become suspicious?

After Gein's capture, when he claimed that he had never shot a deer, there were many who remembered in horror the packs of 'venison' Gein had given them, and the fresh liver he had handed out.

And then I had a piece of luck. In a distant newspaper office I was asked if I had tried Dr Arndt.

Who he?

George Arndt, it turned out, was an eminent psychiatrist who lived just sixty miles from Plainfield, in Neenah, a small town beside Lake Winnebago. These days he was semi-retired, but he had been interested in the Gein case throughout his career.

I called and he was delighted to talk. I discovered that he had been fascinated by the Gein case ever since he had first heard of it in 1957, and had become very close to it, spending months examining Gein along with another psychiatrist when Gein petitioned unsuccessfully for his release from mental hospital in the early Seventies.

George Arndt told me he was working at a hospital in Topeka, Kansas, when Gein was caught. He was struck by the large number of sick jokes the case inspired, which became known as Geiners. There were jokes about cannibalism, sexual perversion or both. He reeled a few off for me. For instance: 'As the host said to late-arriving guests, "Sorry you weren't a little earlier – everyone's eaten."' Or how about: 'What did Gein say to the sheriff who arrested him? "Have a heart."' Or, a little more risqué this one: 'There were no mice around Gein's farmhouse because there were too many pussies.'

In bars, Dr Arndt discovered, drinkers would order Gein beer – with plenty of body but no head. Children reworded a well-known Christmas carol to run 'Deck the walls with limbs of Molly.'

That Christmas, when he returned to his home state of Wisconsin, he found everyone telling such jokes: 'A nephew in the fourth grade, the banker, the insurance man, nearly everyone I ran into would try to outdo each other with their Geiners.'

Arndt realized he had found a subject for the third-year paper he had to write as part of his residency at the Winter General Veterans Hospital. It was published as 'Community Reactions to a Horrifying Event.'

He found that right across the country people were telling Geiners – everywhere except for a twenty-mile radius around Plainfield. While locals reacted with extreme horror and indignation, beyond the immediate vicinity anger and denial were replaced with grim humour. And the joking was so common that Dr Arndt characterized it as a mass repetition compulsion.

'The way people were responding was fascinating. Seemingly the nearby states could look at us and laugh. If you see someone fall in the street right by you, you don't laugh, you help them up. But someone seeing this from a block away might laugh at the sight of a person taking a pratfall.'

In Plainfield, Dr Arndt explained, the reaction was also different because people's deep-seated faith in their fellow man was shattered. The inhabitants of such small towns were used to thinking of their neighbours as stoic, reliable, conscientious, strongly religious. They knew, and felt they could vouch for, everyone in town. Gein was a friend or acquaintance to many: he was a handyman, a carpenter, a babysitter. A nice quiet man. Children especially liked him.

'The Gein case has fascinated me right through my career,' Dr Arndt told me. 'At the time he was certainly America's most bizarre murderer. Not since the holocaust had something been this bizarre, this gross, and this unusual.'

In 1968 Gein was deemed fit to be tried for the killing of Bernice Worden, convicted of first-degree murder but found not guilty by reason of insanity. He was returned to the Central State Hospital for the Insane in Waupun, Wisconsin.

At the trial a good deal came out about his background and possible motivations. Gein had never married, and claimed never to have had sex with a woman. His father, George, who died in 1940, was given to drunken rages and had threatened him and his mother. After his mother suffered a stroke Gein had nursed her. After a second stroke killed her in 1945 he began to experience lapses of memory. He would hear his mother's voice as he fell asleep and developed a belief that he could raise people from the dead through will-power. The grave-robbing could have been motivated by his abnormally close attachment to his mother. He may have been seeking a substitute for her in the form of a replica or body that could be kept indefinitely. He seemed to think of the bodies that surrounded him as being like dolls. Their presence seemed to comfort him.

Gein was obsessed with the idea of becoming a woman himself. In 1952 Christine Jorgensen had created an international sensation when it was revealed that this twenty-six-year-old, blonde, blue-eyed glamour girl had been born a man. Having lived for some years as a male transvestite, she had gone to Copenhagen for a sex-change operation, which could not be performed legally in the United States at the time. Gein was fascinated with the case.

In court, he expressed disapproval of Mary Hogan and Bernice Worden. The first was a dirty talker, he said. He disapproved of her operating a tavern and had heard she was in some crooked business. He believed Bernice Worden wooed her husband away from another girl and married him shortly after the forsaken girl committed suicide. He also believed Bernice had broken up another marriage.

In the early Seventies, Dr Arndt told me, he was one of two psychiatrists appointed by Judge Robert Gollmar to assess Gein when he sought to petition for his own release. He spent many days with him in 1972, '73 and '74, and again in 1980 and '81 when he was to be moved from the high-security hospital for the criminally insane to a normal mental hospital.

'He was not unusual to look at and talk to. He was literally one of the many patients down there at the central state hospital for the criminally insane, a typical individual. If you had not known about his notoriety you would certainly not have picked him out of a crowd. That would go along with the local community's view of him, and the fact that he existed there [in Plainfield] for so long.'

'Was he insane?' I asked.

'He was different, let's put it like that. He had been hospitalized for nearly fifteen years when I saw him. If there was an illness, many times these things get covered over, burned out or go into remission. But it was apparent this was someone who should stay in the hospital. He would be unable to function after fifteen years in an institution and there was also the danger of people wanting revenge.

'He was very limited on what he would be willing to say about the crimes. He did not want to deal with the issues raised by what he had done, or talk to me about what had occurred. I don't think it's ever going to be known why he did this. I've done as much as I could. What we have is what we have. I don't think we can speculate much beyond that.'

Had he been to Plainfield?

'Oh sure, I was the medical psychiatric clinical director of the mental health system of that county, Waushara, for twenty years. I've seen a lot of the people, had a lot of contact, been out and seen the various places and the unusualness of it. Plainfield!' he said, and chuckled. 'What a name!'

At last I was on Gein's trail. Dr Arndt told me where to find his farm. That afternoon, on what happened to be the anniversary of the killing of Bernice Worden, I drove out to the melancholy area of rough scrub and marsh to see the Gein place, or what remains of it.

The day was no longer bright, making the bitter cold hard to endure. Today all that remains of the farm is a clearing with woodland on two sides of it. There was part of a shed among the trees. I found the basement, full of leaves and rubbish, and a few boards from the woodshed, once attached to the house, where Mrs Worden's body was discovered, and traces of the kitchen.

After Gein's capture the place attracted a good deal of ghoulish attention. College kids came out to have all-night parties where they would scare each other witless. Others came for souvenirs. On 30 March 1958 the house was to have been auctioned, and there were plans to turn it into a house-of-horror tourist attraction. But on 27 March it was burned down, allegedly by locals in an early attempt to obliterate the memory of Gein. What escaped the fire was sold, though. A '38 Chevy truck used to carry Mary Hogan's body went for $215, and the maroon Ford in which Bernice Worden's body was brought out to the farm fetched $760, after fierce bidding from fifteen people. It went on display at county fairs under a banner reading 'See Ed Gein's grave-robbing and murder car. $1,000 reward if not true!'

I felt distinctly uneasy out at this place. It was getting dark. What if my car would not start? I drove back to town, and to the cemetery on a side road just before Highway 51.

After his death, on 26 July 1984, Gein was buried here, alongside his mother, father and brother. The headstone bore the marks of the chisels used by ghoulish visitors to chip bits off it. It was in this graveyard that, sometimes within yards of his mother's plot, Gein had robbed graves. I found the names of some of them: Sherman, Adams, Bergstrom, Everson, Sparks, Woodward.

On the south side of the graveyard, two-thirds of the way back, was the Worden family plot. In front of the big central grey stone bearing the surname were the small individual stones and on one of them the inscription: Bernice – 1957.

I strolled round the cemetery, my feet crunching on the frozen ground covered with a dusting of snow, thinking about the difference in the reaction to Gein locally, and further afield. During my trawl through newspapers I had discovered, in the *New London Chronicle*, a rather glib outline of how those who lived a little way away from Plainfield would try and comfort themselves by arguing that such a thing could not happen in their own small town. It was headed: 'New London publisher tells of wildness and mystery in "mad butcher" region:

'Western Waushara county as it melts into the "dead heart" region of Wisconsin centering through Adams and Jackson counties takes on a peculiar, lonely, wild feeling. A feeling of people struggling just for subsistence. A feeling that an honest living is hard to come by in this throbbingly poor area . . . In this back country a common term for its inhabitants is "marsh angels" . . .

'It is on the eastern fringes of this "dead heart" region that the macabre murder setting took place. Even as a youth in Almond just five miles east of where the dead heart region starts in Pottage County we could feel the mystery of that wild marsh and woods country. We knew the rule there was to disregard game laws. We knew that moonshiners worked that desolate area . . . And always and down through the years that area has been burned into our memories as wild, willingly not law-abiding, poor.

'And so when this murder took place on the border of that netherland, it was something we'd suspect would take place, should take place. People seemed to have a disconcern about what other people, even their neighbors, do. Their own struggles are sufficient for their capacities. And if something strange and odd takes place it is much more likely to be accepted

192

as their business and nobody else's . . . it is sort of like a half-wolf, half-dog area where the wolf takes over here, the dog takes over there. But always coming out of the dead-heart area is the everlasting mood of wildness and mystery. And we suspect the lonely 51-year-old bachelor now being held in the Waushara county jail at Wautoma was held to that spell of wildness. Where he was alone. Would be left alone. Where the laws of man were obliterated by the constant and encroaching frontier of wilderness. Where a man could kill a person and clean it like he would a deer . . . This is where murder like that Gein carried out would be most likely to spawn.'

Oh really?

That night in the Johnson Inn I thought some more about this. After his supper Burrell came and talked to me, to the slow ticking of the clock, about the potato-packaging warehouse he managed, about the rhythms of the Plainfield year, planting the potatoes, beans, corn and peppers in May, harvesting them in September, hunting different things at different times. Deer for the next ten days – there were 900,000, plenty for everyone with a gun. Before bed Nancy asked me would it be French toast, stewed fruit, and eggs and ham for breakfast? That sounded fine.

No, I decided as I went upstairs to unwrap a kiss to dream on, the idea that Gein's crimes were more likely to happen in Plainfield than anywhere else had to be nonsense. They could happen anywhere. As Robert Bloch wrote, in an article called 'The Shambles of Ed Gein': 'Men like Ed Gein can be found anywhere in the world – quiet little men leading quiet little lives, smiling their quiet little smiles and dreaming their quiet little dreams . . . the real chamber of horrors is the grey twisted pulsating blood-flecked interior of the human mind.'

And Dr Arndt told me that he believed the story had been turned into hugely affecting and successful films because Gein's crime was an archetypal one which everyone in the world would be affected by, and which hence made such powerful popular entertainment.

'Its horrors spontaneously occurred,' he said. 'It is the old adage that truth is stranger than fiction.' And Ed Gein is the strangest of Strange Angels.

CHAPTER ELEVEN

All The President's Bullets

JOHN F. KENNEDY,
DALLAS, TEXAS, 22 NOVEMBER

Dan was having problems with his bullets. He had lost one of them. There should have been nine, but he had counted them off on his fingers and only got to eight. He counted them off again. The crowd grew restless. A couple sniggered at him.

Bullets matter. Bullets are at the very centre of things. Bullets are what bring so many people to Dealey Plaza in Dallas: the scene, on 22 November 1963, of the assassination of President John Fitzgerald Kennedy. On the eve of the thirtieth anniversary of the killing there were several thousand people in town, many of them sporting a black name tag bearing a large question mark, which identified them as attending something called the Assassination Symposium on John F. Kennedy.

Officially there were only three bullets, all fired by Lee Harvey Oswald from his sniper's nest on the sixth floor of the Texas Schoolbook Depository. Three means the official line, that President Kennedy was killed by a lone assassin, can be held. Even four bullets blows the whole thing open, because it means that there had to be a second gunman, and hence some kind of conspiracy.

Nine bullets is extreme even by the standards of the thousands of proponents of a hundred conflicting conspiracy theories, theories that pin the blame on the CIA, the FBI, the Mafia, left-wing Americans, right-wing Cubans, some combination of any or all of the above, or even onto Lyndon Johnson, Richard Nixon, and George Bush.

Dan Stevens had a uniquely complex theory as to the actual mechanics of the killing, and with his booming delivery he soon gathered a crowd interested to hear what it was. Strutting along the front of the white concrete pergola on Dealey Plaza, from which the grass slopes down to Elm Street and the spot at which the assassination took place, he said, 'I think there were three hit teams.' He paused for effect, pushed his sun-reactive glasses up his nose, tugged at the lapels of his blue nylon jacket on which he wore a British Military Police badge, and explained. 'One behind the fence here, behind the area that has become known as the grassy knoll, one on the sixth floor of the book depository and one on the second floor of the building across the street beyond the book depository, the Dal-Tex building.

'There were four gunmen. Two back here behind the fence, one up there in the depository and one over there in the Dal-Tex. There were nine shots. Five hits. Four misses.'

Dan does not believe Oswald fired a shot.

He has been relating his assassination theory six days a week for the past two years on this spot: accosting anyone who will listen and selling copies of his $3 newspaper, *JFK Today*, which he confesses is actually little more than a tourist brochure. He is one of half a dozen hawkers of Kennedy-assassination theories who work the crowds – rarely fewer than a couple of hundred, sometimes over a thousand strong – that come daily to Dealey Plaza. A 1930s municipal park, the plaza is dissected by three roads that squeeze under a triple railway underpass at the bottom of the hill, fan out as they climb across the site and feed into downtown Dallas.

'OK, now, for your first shot,' he said, getting into the meat of the thing. 'There is a guy standing on the grassy knoll who hears a gunshot behind him, a bullet goes by just to the west of him and he can feel the wind. That's the first shot. It hits Kennedy in the throat right here,' and he prodded a forefinger to his Adam's apple, turning through a half-circle as he did so, so that everyone could see. 'It is a low-calibre weapon, designed entirely just to shut him up. This keeps him from saying help or anything.

'The second hits the kerb eight feet out from the triple underpass. The third bullet hits Governor John Connally, who was sitting directly in front of Kennedy, in the right shoulder. The fourth hits the chrome above the rear-view mirror. The fifth hits the windshield. The sixth hits Kennedy in the back. The seventh hits the sidewalk. The eighth blows the brains out the back of Kennedy's head.'

Dan paused. 'That's only eight,' he said in puzzlement. 'Let's count 'em again.' He did. It was still eight. 'I missed a shot in here somewhere, anyways that's eight, that's good enough!' And he turned and walked away from the crowd in some agitation.

The crowd dispersed, off to hear other theories.

A little later Dan found me again. He was still very agitated about his missing bullet. 'I hope I did OK,' he said, like an actor who feared he had failed an audition. 'I forgot the final shot, the one that hits Connally in the right wrist and the left thigh.'

So then there were nine.

I had got into town the previous night, and from the moment I touched down I had felt ill. A nagging pain in my back which had developed during my flight from Los Angeles was exacerbated as I climbed into my hire car. As I drove the pain got worse. When I arrived at my hotel I had to press my palms flat on the counter as I was checked in, then brace myself for the ride in the elevator and the walk to my room. By the time I got there I was in real agony. I tried lying flat out on the bed but that didn't help. I went and got painkillers from the hotel vending machine but they did no good

197

either, although I took three times the recommended dose. In the early hours, out of desperation, I ran a hot bath and sat in that. Finally, after an hour or so of soaking in water as hot as I could bear, the pain subsided and I was able to sleep.

But next morning as I walked around Dealey Plaza I felt decidedly delicate and particularly intolerant of conspiracy theorists. Their theorizing seemed so irrelevant. Even if one of them happened to hit upon the truth they could never prove it. And there were so many theories being propounded that to walk through the Plaza was like wading through conspiracy soup.

The striking thing about the place was how familiar it was, although I had never been there. I could find my way around the main landmarks – the book depository and the grassy knoll, with the pergola in between – just as easily as I could close my eyes and picture the layout of the first house I lived in, though I have not been back to it for twenty-seven years. Dealey Plaza was a place in my past, in everyone's past. And looking from the pergola to the streets I could see instantly how the Kennedy limousine had come down the middle road – Main Street – turned right along Houston, and then doglegged left into Elm, to pass right before me.

This sense that the assassination was a part of everyone's past was what drew the many thousands of visitors every year. It is a past they feel they have to confront.

I half expected to find the foremost Kennedy obsessive in America here on the eve of the thirtieth anniversary of JFK's assassination. I looked around but could not see him. Bill Clinton was still in the White House. And though, on the grassy knoll, there were rumours that he would be here in the morning for the ceremony marking the anniversary, and the dedication of Dealey Plaza as a site of national historic significance, he did not show. Instead he went to Arlington cemetery, where an eternal flame burns on the grave of John F. Kennedy.

But I had noted with interest over the past few months that, as the anniversary approached, Bill Clinton had been showing all the signs I had seen in many other obsessives as they prepare for a highly significant anniversary connected with their hero, their role model, the person they would like to be.

Of course, from the moment he entered the presidential race, comparisons were made between Clinton and Kennedy. There was nothing special about that. It is part of the normal, cynical political game for a politician to seize every opportunity to link himself to his party's last successful president, to seek to appeal to memories of a time when Americans still believed in politicians. Kennedy is often described as the last president America trusted. And, as it would dearly love to trust again, there were plenty of people looking to Clinton and hoping that he would turn out to have something of the character and charisma of that giant Jack Kennedy.

At that point, there was nothing out of the ordinary in the fact that Clinton's inauguration was packed with allusion to Kennedy. Obviously the meeting on the White House lawn in 1963, when seventeen-year-old Bill Clinton shook hands with Kennedy, had made an indelible impression on him. And why not? Even a president needs heroes. Maybe there is also nothing out of the ordinary in the fact that Clinton tracked down the desk Kennedy used and had it returned to the Oval Office, where he now worked at it. But in the months leading up to the anniversary of the assassination, Clinton's obsession snowballed.

He spent his 1993 summer holiday with the Kennedy clan in Martha's Vineyard, the Cape Cod island close to the Kennedy family compound at Hyannis Port, and went sailing with his widow, Jacqueline Kennedy Onassis.

In the months before the anniversary, Clinton made a point of speaking at an obscure river wharf in New Orleans, at Washington's American University and at

199

the University of North Carolina – all places where Kennedy made important appearances thirty years earlier. Like those who follow James Dean's death drive, he was tracking his hero's final movements.

In early November, he joined the Kennedy family for the re-dedication of the revamped Kennedy Library in Boston, and made a speech in which he sought to draw parallels between his own fledgling National Service Program and Kennedy's much-admired Peace Corps, between his support for a pared-down space station and Kennedy's drive to put the first man on the moon.

At the library ceremony the Kennedy family presented him with a leatherbound collection of JFK's writings and Kennedy's last surviving brother, Edward, uttered words that must have filled him with elation: 'My brother would have been proud of you,' he said, 'and so are we.' It was as if one of the candle-bearing fans in vigil at Graceland on the anniversary of Elvis's death had been singled out by his widow, Priscilla Presley, and been told: 'Elvis would have been touched by your devotion. Please do everything you can to keep his name alive.'

During 1993 Clinton seemed to become an honorary member of the Kennedy family. He must have felt like those fans of Marilyn who get such a buzz from talking to someone who knew their idol, someone who, through their first-hand recollections of the adored individual, can turn them from dry death to living flesh. He reminded me of Ruth, whom I had met at Marilyn's grave, or Michelle in Reno, who believes she was infused by Marilyn's spirit shortly after her death.

Clinton reads all the books, like any other obsessive follower of Elvis or Marilyn or Dean or Kennedy. Just before the anniversary he was reading *President Kennedy: A Profile in Power* by Richard Reeves, and invited the author to lunch in the White House.

White House watchers say – the presidency being such a lonely job – that there is nothing unusual in a president communing with a past incumbent. The more cynical liken it to a dwarf basking in the reflected glory of a giant. Those who have grave doubts about Clinton's abilities put it down less to a desire for reflected glory than to a weak leader's search for an identity. But maybe, if the widespread devotion to dead heroes is a pervasive modern malaise, Clinton is simply a part of that malaise. It does seem unfortunate, however, that the leader of the free world should be obsessed by a dead man.

There is another prominent man trapped in the shadow of JFK, and that is his son, John Jnr. At the time of the thirtieth anniversary of his father's death, the newspapers were full of articles about the good-looking John and his actress girlfriend Daryl Hannah. They talked of the couple being 'perfect casting for the revival of Camelot' and asked if the extraordinarily glamorous heir could revive the magic of his father's brief three-year reign. A book about him was entitled *Prince Charming*. *People* magazine called him the sexiest man alive. He was America's answer to the Princess of Wales – but without the eating disorders and the jug-eared party-pooper.

This wishful thinking had its genesis in one photograph of such iconic potency that he could never escape from it. It showed him, on the day of his father's funeral, 25 November, which also happened to be his third birthday, standing in a little blue coat outside St Matthew's Cathedral, his right arm raised in salute to his dead father. No-one who saw that picture, and hundreds of millions did, could ever forget it. John Jnr was trapped for ever as his murdered father's son.

From that moment there would be a million dreams that he would grow up to take on his father's mantle, restore the idyll which was shattered by assassination, give America back its hope, dignity and idealism. He would make a frumpy middle-aged nation feel young, alive, vibrant, right and good once more.

He has yet to show any sign of doing so.

Inevitably, his passage was not a smooth one. John Jnr was a disruptive, hyperactive schoolboy, a poor student who experimented with drugs and whose one great passion – apart from women – was for acting, which his mother discouraged. His best friend was his cousin, William Kennedy Smith, son of JFK's sister Jean, who would later be controversially acquitted of rape in Palm Beach in 1991. He went to law school after graduation, and failed his Bar exams twice before eventually qualifying and becoming an assistant district attorney in Manhattan.

So, the theory goes, Kennedy was not the only victim in Dealey Plaza. His son John and the other young members of the Kennedy clan are victims also, trapped and mesmerized by the Kennedy image. Bobby's son Joe Jnr, named after Bobby's father, has tried to live up to an ideal which was largely illusory. As a congressman he has taken on his father's political stance but seems to lack something at his core. David, who died after a long battle with drink and drugs in 1984, and Bobby Jnr, who barely survived heroin addiction, appear to have succumbed to the pressure of the image.

In a way, I thought, as I wandered between the conspiracy theorists at the grassy knoll, we are all in the shadow of the Kennedy assassination.

At Dealey Plaza the defenders of the theory of Oswald as lone assassin were few and far between. There was a strong sense of anger lifting like steam from the huddles of Kennedy tourists listening to the theorists, or 'members of the research community' as they like to be known. Most believed they had been lied to. And they were mad about it. I, as a seven-year-old boy, had been lied to, Bill Clinton had been lied to. And the way the Kennedy reign came to an end before he was exposed as a weak, vacillating, obsessive womanizer, meant that we were in the thrall of an illusion. No-one could say a word against Kennedy – certainly not here. It was a form of mass escapism. The continued belief in the Kennedy myth marked the rejection of the uninspiring present in favour of a retreat into a falsely comforting past. This, at any rate, is my view. But everyone was here to see for themselves.

Visitors were trying out the locations. A steady trickle awaited their turn to stand up on the low wall before the pergola on which the most famous home movie of all time was shot. Here, a thirty-eight-year-old Dallas dress manufacturer called Abraham Zapruder stood with his 8mm home-movie camera and filmed Kennedy's head snapping back as if shot from in front. They wanted to capture the same scene with their camcorders.

Back behind the fence at the rear of the grassy knoll an ever-changing crowd was taking its own camera pot-shots and debating what happened here.

'If you stand flat-footed the wall's an obstacle,' one was saying.

'Keep in mind, now, his head was not on the street,' another replied. 'His head was up in the limousine, so the wall wouldn't matter.'

In the car park behind the grassy knoll the TV news satellite trucks were arriving ready for tomorrow's dedication ceremony, their dishes being raised to the heavens. Other visitors were darting through the traffic to stand and be photographed in the centre lane of Elm, on the very spot where the President took the fatal shot. Inconspicuous on the edge of the grass alongside the spot was a red wreath, lying before a piece of board which covered a plaque. This would be unveiled tomorrow, when the spot would be declared a site of national historic significance.

The debates meandered on, as they do every day in Dealey Plaza, as yet more people spend yet more hours considering an incident that lasted just six seconds. Those six seconds are the most studied and disputed in American history, spawning 600 books and countless conspiracy theories. Conspiracy was like a religion for these people, who resembled the followers of a hundred fragmented sects. As with religious belief, adherents of two opposing theories could not be swayed by argument or science. The truth could never be known, no one theory could be proven or disproven. There was no such thing as objective evidence. Each group rejected information that threatened its position, or sifted it in such a way that anything which weakened its position was lost, anything that supported it was enhanced. Conflict and confusion would reign for ever. Those who believe the researchers are clawing their way towards some final solution to the Kennedy assassination puzzle are wrong. We will never know.

What is clear is that belief in the official version of events is diminishing. The Warren Commission, set up in 1964 by Lyndon B. Johnson to put an end to speculation, did no such thing. An opinion poll conducted straight after its findings were published showed only 56 per cent of Americans accepted its conclusion that Oswald acted alone. In 1991, another poll found that this figure had fallen to 11 per cent.

'Every now and then they come down here in tears,' said Dan, who had found me again. 'A lot come down just to have their picture made, but they nearly all leave with kind of a bitter taste in their mouths, especially if they go up to the Sixth Floor and see that farce and then come down here and hear the truth.'

The Sixth Floor is a museum, created on the floor of the depository from which Oswald is supposed to have acted. I went there next. The exhibition I saw is subtitled 'John F. Kennedy and the Memory of a Nation', and that's what it is really about. It is much more of a record of the Kennedy years and how the world reacted to his death than it is an investigation into the circumstances of the killing. As far as responsibility for the death, it pretty much holds the Oswald-did-it line, but does record the fact that in 1978 the House Committee on Assassinations concluded that Oswald was part of a conspiracy and suggested there was a 98 per cent probability – or better – that a fourth shot came from the grassy knoll, but that it missed.

The exhibition seeks to set Kennedy in his time. One display entitled The New Generation includes a publicity still from Alfred Hitchcock's *Psycho*, another from *Breakfast at Tiffany's*, the album cover to Bob Dylan's *Freewheelin'* and others by Chubby Checker and Andy Williams. The bookshop has a novel volume called '*John F. Kennedy and his family – Paper Dolls In Full Colour*', which enables you to dress and undress him, Jackie and the kids. I was beginning to think I'd rather play with that than hear another conspiracy theory.

There were several affecting film-loops playing on a series of TV screens around the museum. One was of Walter Cronkite announcing the death thirty-eight minutes after it was confirmed and struggling to keep his emotions in check. Elsewhere the Zapruder film looped endlessly. The goriest moments, when something horrible grows from the President's head, had been cut out, but it was still numbing, the effect heightened rather than lessened by its repetition. This film must constantly play in hell. Another film-loop was of Oswald being shot by Ruby, his face scrunching up as the bullet enters his side. These images will remain in my head for ever.

If anything, the sense of anger was even stronger up here. 'This is where they want us to believe the shot was fired,' said a woman, standing beside the glassed-off corner of the floor, in which a pile of boxes screen the half-opened window from which Oswald is supposed to have fired. 'You know why it's glassed off?' asked her friend. 'So you can't see what a hard shot it was.'

A queue of people waited to write in the visitors' books, three large ring binders, the clean white sheets of which were rapidly filled with angry scrawls. People seemed to need to record something, even if they had nothing to communicate. 'It was my tenth birthday,' read one entry, leaving what the killing had meant unsaid. 'You can never trust a politician but you can trust JFK' said another, ignoring the evidence which has built up in the years since the assassination to raise doubts about that statement. 'It was an honour to come here and be part of history.' 'If you can shed any light on a case that has been driving people crazy for 30 years, you must do it.'

Among the researchers the greatest hunger is for contact with those who were here in Dealey Plaza on the fateful day. Witnesses are the most valued and esteemed relic. To hear them speak was to touch the reality, like dipping your finger in the President's blood.

And today many of them were here. They had been brought together for the Kennedy Symposium, two days of theorizing which over a thousand 'members of the research community' had paid $50 to take part in. On the other side of Dealey Plaza, in the mirror-glass silos of the Hyatt Regency, the witnesses were having lunch. They were eating in the hotel's tower-top restaurant, a glass fist sitting atop a concrete forearm.

Thirty years ago these ordinary people took an early lunch and came down to see their president, only to become part of shocking history. They are celebrities, stars, and this afternoon they would tell their stories once again. They would come and stand on Dealey Plaza in the same spots where they stood thirty years ago, except that this time they would have a microphone in their hands. We would meet the people who had become known as the Babushka Lady and the Deaf Mute, we would hear of the Lady in Red, the Umbrella Man and the Cuban.

I went over to the symposium, where a trade mart was going strong in a room the size of a sports hall. It was packed with all kinds of products and theories.

'JFK Assassination Solved!' trumpeted one stall, offering the answers on a $29 video. Another had T-shirts which read: 'Jail Bush for the Murder of JFK'.

Those who believe Oswald killed Kennedy must also believe in the so-called 'magic bullet'. This bullet is said to have been responsible for five wounds in Kennedy and Connally but to have survived, totally undamaged, to be discovered by investigators.

You can buy a magic bullet, pristine in a plastic pouch, together with a replica of a bullet that has been fired through the wrist of a human cadaver. The fired bullet has a flattened nose and is intended to show that causing one wound, let alone five, does a lot to deform a projectile. Did that magic, undamaged bullet smash through two men's bodies and come out looking like this? People shake their heads. And buy.

Among the assorted wares I saw an assassination calendar, with one sicko picture of a murder for each month of the year, not just of JFK – Mr November – but Lincoln, Bobby Kennedy, John Lennon and others. And there were endless books, audiotapes and videos for sale. Did a spy assume Oswald's identity? Want a taped interview with the employer of Jack Ruby, the man who killed Oswald? Or maybe, at $20 for four, some colour pictures of the presidential limousine in which Kennedy was killed? It was refurbished, made bulletproof and is now in the Ford car museum in Detroit.

I moved around this hall of mirrors and met a little guy on crutches standing beside an easel. He gave me his card, which identified him as W. Blaine Scudder, historian and cryptanalyst. On the easel was a sheet of paper covered with columns of letters. At the top was the name Alek James Hidell. Beneath each letter of the name was a column of twenty-six letters, each column beginning with the next letter in the alphabet to the letter in the name to which it corresponded, so that after twenty-six lines the final line on the sheet was back to Alek James Hidell once more.

Hidell was an alias used by Oswald – for purchasing the rifle with which he is supposed to have murdered Kennedy among other things – for ten months before the assassination, Scudder told me. What we had here, he went on, was a cryptogram. Picked out on the columns in yellow highlighter pen were any sequences of letters which made up words, or pseudo words: DO JKF PATZY NOV TEXD STOP.

Scudder's theory was that the alias Alek James Hidell was given to Oswald by his controllers in Military Intelligence. The alias, he said, was a lock. The cryptogram which could be derived from it was the key. Oswald knew something of cryptology, said Scudder, and he found the key to the lock. When he had unlocked this message he found out what he was being set up for. He realized that Kennedy would be killed, he would be done, hence the word DO. JKF is almost JFK, thereby identifying the victim. Oswald, or Hidell, would be the patsy (PATZY was almost the correct spelling, close enough to be recognized). It would happen in November (NOV) in Dallas, Texas (TEXD), and JFK would be stopped (hence STOP).

'Now Lee had, in the last moments of his life, figured this message out and realized he had been set up,' said Scudder. 'And that's why, on national TV, he said "I'm just a patsy." This was the only means he had available to him, considering he was in Dallas County lock-up, to make his innocence known. As the last rational act of a desperate man he tried to get a clue out, hoping to God above that someone would realize that he was set up.

'The controller who heard him use the word patsy would know he had to be got rid of. As soon as Lee said "I'm just a patsy," whoever was controlling Jack Ruby knew that he had to die. Oswald knew that in saying what he did he could be signing his own death warrant. That was obviously on his mind when, on the morning of November 24, when he was being escorted from his cell to the elevator, he turned to officer Jim Levell and made the statement "nobody's going to shoot me in here." Less than five minutes later that is exactly what happened. I don't think he was a gunman at all and as far as I'm concerned this establishes it. Military Intelligence gave Lee this name and set him up from the word go.'

When the star witnesses assembled on Dealey Plaza for an action replay of the tragedy, only the principal victim was missing.

Someone had drawn a length of yellow and black tape across the top of Elm and the traffic was being funnelled round to Main. Now we could stand on the exact assassination spot without having to dodge the traffic. Dan slapped down a copy of a book called *When They Kill a President* so we could be sure we had the right place.

The press of bodies was huge as the master of ceremonies, Larry Ray Harris, wearing an 'Oswald Was a Patsy' badge, struggled through the crowd with a microphone, followed by a man carrying a PA speaker on a tripod, to set the scene for the witnesses. Harris introduced 'The single most important living eyewitness to the assassination (and definitely the prettiest) Beverley Oliver-Massegee – the Babushka Lady.' This nickname, I gathered, was due to the fur coat that Beverley wore on the fatal day.

She was a big blonde Southern girl in a pink jacket, deeply tanned and with corkscrew curls tumbling over her shoulders. She got a great welcome. This was the real thing at last. The crowd was silent for her speech.

'I was an entertainer at the Colony Club in downtown Dallas. It was separated by a parking lot from Jack Ruby's infamous Carousel Club. Jack and I became very personal friends through the years. Yes, I was only seventeen years old that November 22 1963 but I had been working in Dallas since about fourteen and on November 22 I came down to this spot to see my beloved President, JFK. I was excited. The air was absolutely charged with electricity. I had a brand new movie camera and I started filming to make sure I knew how to use it. As the motorcade turned onto Elm there was some noises. I assume they were bullets. As the President's car got just past me there was a loud b-boom and the President went violently back against the seat. It looked as though somebody had thrown a bucket of blood out the back of his head, and I was frozen and suspended in time. To a degree I am still frozen and suspended in time, because I live with that nightmare every day of my life.

'So I went home. I took two Tuinals and I went to bed. That evening early my mom insisted I bring her back down here to see the flowers. I questioned her wisdom because she knew what I was going through, but I brought her here, and we took pictures. The next day she wanted to come down again. We took pictures of the flowers again. I didn't go to work Friday night, or Saturday night, and – of course – I didn't go to work Sunday night because, as you know, Sunday morning my friend Jack Ruby went into the basement of the police department and he blew away a man who he had introduced to me two or three weeks prior as his friend Lee Oswald, with the CIA.

'At seventeen years old I did not know what the CIA was. I was not impressed. And I must be honest, I'm still not sure what the CIA is.' (Laughter.) 'And I'm still not impressed.' (Whoops and applause.)

'I was very frightened, I was very confused because then I'm hearing reports that the President was shot from the back of the head. Now I know I'm blonde, I know that I'm dumb, but I'm going to tell you what, I'm not stupid. And I know from going hunting with my brother Eugene Oliver that when something is shot the body movement goes in the direction of the trajectory of the bullet. My President went violently backwards, he never went forward until Jackie pulled him forward, she pushed him down and she climbed over the back

210

to get whatever it was on the back of the trunk which I believe to be brain matter.

'I went back to work at 7.45 on November 25. There were two men waiting on the landing of our club. A tall man with a stetson and a big cleft in his chin stepped forward. He had a badge and an ID card. He told me he was with the FBI. He wanted to know if I had been at the grassy place taking pictures the day Kennedy was killed. He said he wanted my film and as it was in my make-up case I gave it to him. He said he wanted to get it developed and look at it for evidence and we will get it back to you in a few days.

'Why did I turn that film over? Because lying right next to it was a Prince Albert can full of grade-A marijuana. In 1959 a very famous stripper by the name of Candy Bar was sentenced to fifteen years in the penitentiary for less than an ounce. If that man had asked me for my soul that day I would have tried to give it to him. I was not smart enough to ask for a receipt. I have held the hope in my heart for many years that they would bring my film back to me. It hasn't been returned as of today but I'm still hoping.'

Behind the crowd came the whoop of a police siren. When we turned we saw a lone black policeman standing at the open door of his patrol car in the middle of Elm. Through a loudhailer he said, 'People will you please leave. This is an unauthorized road closure, you have to get off the street.'

He was ignored, as we shuffled further down the slope and were introduced to Wayne and Edna Hartman.

'We were in town for a friend's trial,' said Mr Hartman. 'We heard shots so we came down to the point where we heard them and we were looking at the ground in this area and my wife said "Look, there's a mole hole going back here." We followed it back for 8 feet with a policeman and my wife said

"Boy that's a big mole hole and look how far it goes."
The policeman said "No that's a bullet hole." We told
the FBI this but when we got verification of the story
as they had written it up it had been changed. We
told the FBI the shot could not have come from up
there' (he pointed to the book depository) 'because the
mark was going back this way' (he pointed towards
the grassy knoll). 'But in the report they said it came
from the book depository. I don't know where they got
their story from but it is certainly not what we told
them.'

The policeman was getting impatient. 'Can I have
your attention?' he asked.

'Oh no, no,' was the answer.

'We got to clear this street, we need you to get off the
street.'

'Can't you go arrest a drug dealer or something?' A
young black-haired guy was squaring up to the cop.
An earnest-looking woman pushed past me. ''Scuse
me, 'scuse me,' she said, 'I have to get through. I'm a
barrister.'

So far the altercation had been light-hearted. There
were calls of 'I am not resisting arrest' and 'I'm just
a patsy', but people refused to move, and it looked
as if it could turn nasty. Several people were now
squaring up to the cop, prodding at him with their
fingers. He got back into his car and picked up his
radio handset.

While he did so we were introduced to Malcolm
Summers, who seemed a little put off by the commotion. 'I was at the post office annexe over here,'
he said. 'I run across the top of the grassy knoll here, I
been there five minutes when they came by. I heard the
first shot, the third was much louder, their car stopped
momentarily right there at my spot and I heard Jackie
Kennedy say "Oh God no" and I heard Connally say
"They are going to kill us all."

'It was a very sad thing to hear. It was a sad day for
Dallas and I'm sorry it happened here,' adding, as if

fearful that this last remark did not smack of Southern hospitality, 'thank y'all for coming though.'

The police had sent reinforcements. Three cop cars were now lined up, one in each lane on Elm, their sirens sounding, moving slowly forward, forcing people off the street. Someone yelled out, 'You're messing with the wrong group of people here,' as if it was dangerous to tangle with conspiracy theorists. The crowd moved ahead of the cops as microphone and speaker were taken further down the slope to Ed Hoffman, better known in research circles as the Deaf Mute. On the way we noted the position of Jean Hill, a.k.a. the Lady in Red, who could not be with us today because of sickness, but who had been the closest civilian to the President when he was shot.

We shuffled, too, past the spot at which had stood the two mysterious characters, one who became known as the Umbrella Man, the other as the Cuban. The Umbrella Man had opened and twirled a black umbrella just as the shooting started. Was it a weapon, a signal to the gunmen or, as was claimed by a man – Stephen Witt of Dallas – who came forward fifteen years later and said he was the umbrella man, a taunt to Kennedy that harked back to his father Joseph's support for Neville Chamberlain and his policy of appeasing Hitler? Chamberlain carried a black umbrella, the explanation went, Joseph Kennedy supported his policy, hence the umbrella in Dealey Plaza.

Ed Hoffman, with grey hair, a sandy moustache, glasses and a black blazer, smiled an open-mouthed smile as he too received a hero's welcome, then signed his story, which was spoken by an interpreter. He had been at a vantage point on the Stemmens Freeway beyond the grassy knoll and seen a puff of smoke come up from behind the picket fence. Then he'd seen a man hand a gun to another man, who dismantled it and put it in a tool bag. 'I saw

JFK slump down, it looked like Jello, bloody Jello coming out the back of his head.'

The police were moving in, the crowd was off the road and the traffic flowed down Elm once more. There were mutterings, but the flashpoint had passed, the witness-stars had told their stories, and people dispersed.

That evening the pain came back. I was eating in the Denny's across the street from my motel when it hit me. The waitress, a sweet Hispanic girl, thought I had gone into a seizure as I tried to ease the pain in my back. That night nothing would ease the agony, not painkillers, nor a hot bath. I didn't know what the cause was, but if I had had a weakness for conspiracy theories I might have blamed the CIA, the FBI and the Mafia – or at least somebody who did not want me to write about Kennedy.

One thing I was determined not to do was go to a doctor. At the very least I would probably have to spend the next day being checked over in hospital, so I would miss tomorrow's ceremony. And my travel insurance had run out, so if it did prove to be something serious I could end up with a bill for thousands of dollars. Also, I had been in America for almost four months. I was going home the day after tomorrow. I had a new job on a new newspaper to look forward to. I was not going to miss that plane. Being ill would have to wait.

But that night I was in constant agony. I lay in a hot bath for hours. Early next morning I got the hotel to direct me to a pharmacist, who dosed me up with something that turned my urine bright orange. The girl in Denny's, whom I was beginning to look upon in the way that a dying soldier in the Crimea might have looked upon Florence Nightingale, brought me soup for breakfast, and I headed back to Dealey Plaza.

Great lumbering orange low-loader trucks bearing huge concrete sections had been pulled across the top of Elm, Main and Commerce, the three roads leading to Dealey Plaza. Perhaps they expected an assault from terrorists on tanks. There were police everywhere: on the streets, on the rooftops, in a helicopter. Six cops on mountain bikes were clustered round their sergeant on Houston. He was talking conspiracy, like everyone else in Dallas, and they were listening intently.

Unlike thirty years ago, the cops had the place covered. You could not get behind the picket fence on the grassy knoll, or anywhere near it. You could not get to the sixth floor of the old book-depository building – the place was closed until after the ceremony in Dealey Plaza arranged to mark the anniversary.

On TV, Dr Pepper Jenkins was recalling the awful moment at Parklands Hospital when Jackie Kennedy said to him 'Will this help?' and handed him an object she had retrieved from the rear trunk of the limousine and cradled in her hands during the rush to the hospital.

With pornographic intent the interviewer coaxed him on to say it, say it.

'She handed me a part of the President's brain.'

There, the gory orgasm. Dr Jenkins looked shaken at what he had said.

'It is a bad memory. It has taken me a long time to tell that part of the story.' But, once told, it would lead every bulletin.

On Main Street, a newspaper hawker had found a man who had never heard of JFK. 'Man, I can't believe you never heard of him,' he said. 'What planet you say you was from?'

The man looked in bewilderment at the cordoned-off streets and the crowds massing, waiting to be let down onto Dealey Plaza for the ceremony. It seemed the whole world knew something he didn't.

Two blacks with buckets of red roses were saying buy a rose to place on the grave, as if they believed Kennedy was buried down there in the grass beside Elm.

The board had been removed from the plaque, and

the area roped off. There were piles of flowers, and large yellow flower letters spelling out JFK. The plaza's amphitheatre was filled with a sea of heads. There was a stage at the bottom of the slope before the triple underpass, the central arch of which was covered by a huge Stars and Stripes, screening the route the dying Kennedy took as he was rushed towards Parklands Hospital.

There was not the anger of yesterday, nor the excitement, nor even a sense of occasion. As became clear when the ceremonies got under way, the day had been commandeered by minor civic dignitaries and precocious Dallas schoolchildren.

No Clinton, no Kennedys. The closest to a star was Mrs Nellie Connally, who sat beside her husband in the limousine and had spoken the last words Kennedy heard: 'You sure can't say Dallas doesn't love you, Mr President,' to which he replied, with the last words he would utter: 'No, you can't.'

We got a speech from someone called The Honorable Bob Armstrong, Assistant Secretary for Land and Minerals Management, Department of the Interior, the national anthem sung by Patrice Pike, SBK/EMI recording artist, 1988 graduate, Arts Magnet High School, Dallas, and three kids from Woodrow Wilson High School trilling their way through Kennedy quotations: 'Ask NOT what your country can DO for YOU, ask RATHER what YOU can DO for your COUNTry.'

The programme we were each handed on arrival gave us the words to 'America the Beautiful' and 'Texas Our Texas'.

'Texas our Texas! All hail the mighty State!
Texas our Texas! So wonderful so great!
Boldest and grandest, withstanding every test;
O Empire wide and glorious, you stand supremely blest!'

I haven't been able to stop humming it to myself ever since.

And as if all this wasn't enough, the dumb cops in the helicopter were circling repeatedly overhead, drowning half of what was said. No-one could hear 'The Star Spangled Banner' play as the Stars and Stripes and the flag of Texas, with its lone star, were raised and dutifully unfurled in the light breeze when they reached the top of their poles. And then my view was blocked by someone in a T-shirt emblazoned with the phrase: 'Operation ghetto storm: LA Spring '92' and illustrated with a blazing city over which police helicopters clattered.

Down on the stage someone was saying something about this being a small corner of Dallas that belonged to everyone in the world, but it was hard to be sure, what with everyone else yelling 'Whadda he say?'

Then police-car sirens joined in and the cacophony got worse. There was another speech being made, something about 'I suppose all of us remember . . . and I think millions of Americans . . . 1963 . . . Jack Kennedy . . . his contribution . . . mankind . . . the light flickered but it didn't go out . . .'

The clock was ticking towards 12.30, but there was no crescendo building to the moment. It seemed it would be an anticlimax.

Mrs Connally got lots of applause. At last a witness, someone worth listening to – if you could hear her. 'Thirty years ago today,' she said, 'fate brought me here to witness an unforgettable, tragic event of our time.' Then the helicopter returned and all we got were snippets. 'On behalf of . . . it is my honour . . . historic monument . . . all young people here today will dedicate their lives to preserving . . . thank you.'

The time of the assassination had come and gone without any minute's silence to cover the exact anniversary of the six seconds of the killing. I realized that the assassination had not been mentioned at all in the ceremony unless the chopper had made me miss it.

And now it was over. As people wandered away I went down to look at the plaque, and was surprised to find it did not mention the assassination either. It did not even mention Kennedy. All it said was that the spot was of national historical significance. Others who came to look at the plaque were surprised too. I felt the sense of anger around me again. A woman knelt and placed flowers and a note nearby. The note bore a large red A and went on to ask: 'Who chose not to mention the A word?'

Others read it and murmured their sympathy with its sentiments. Someone beside me said, 'God, they really did the least that they could, didn't they?'

Later my sweet Denny's angel looked at my orange pallor with a wonderful depth of concern (these drugs were dyeing me from the inside out), and brought me more soup. That night the drugs enabled me to sleep and I dreamed of a surprisingly large number of ways in which she was able to make me feel better. I felt quite embarrassed facing her over breakfast the next morning. But then, she was the one who should have been feeling ashamed of herself, if I recall my dream correctly.

There were just a few hours to kill before my plane. The only worry was that the course of drugs was going to run out in mid-Atlantic.

I passed the time before the flight by paying a visit to the other Kennedy museum, called the JFK Assassination Information Center. It is across the street from an empty, wind-blown lot on which stands the Kennedy memorial. The memorial's thirty-foot-high white concrete screen walls enclose a space some twenty feet square, leaving just two narrow slits through which you walk to find, in the centre of an area of barren grey paving-stones, a low slab of black marble. Engraved on its two longer sides is the name John F. Kennedy. It is a strange monument. The screen walls look like something the police might erect to shield a murder site. Within them were bouquets, wreaths and flags, tugged at by the bitter wind that whipped in through the gaps in the screens.

At the JFK Assassination Information Center the banner identifying the museum had flopped down over the door. Inside, a sign propped up on the counter apologized that the exhibits were not ready, and waived the $5 admission fee. It seemed particularly unfortunate that the place should be in such a state of unreadiness on such a significant date. Was this all part of the conspiracy, or were they just incompetent? I suspected the latter.

What little there was to see offered a very different view from that of the Sixth Floor. It took as its starting point the idea that Oswald did not act alone, dug straight into the inconsistencies of the case against him and explored the conspiracy theories. There were blow-ups of photos of Oswald holding the gun with which he is supposed to have killed Kennedy. The intention was to show that the pictures were faked, with Oswald's head stuck on another man's body.

There was a sequence of stills of the Umbrella Man and the Cuban. The Cuban raised his hand and the Umbrella Man his umbrella immediately after the first shot. One minute after the shots the Cuban walked over and sat down beside the Umbrella Man. Moments later the Cuban briefly raised a walkie-talkie to his mouth. The Umbrella Man had hidden his umbrella. The Cuban walked away, tucking the radio into his back pocket, the Umbrella Man went off in the opposite direction. Or did they? So many theories, so much evidence, so much confusion.

I started to wonder about Gene Kelly. He had a black umbrella in *Singin' in the Rain*. And he threw it away when he really needed it. Why? Maybe it wasn't an umbrella at all. Maybe it was a signal.

Yes, I was getting the hang of this conspiracy business. I'd make a member of the research community yet.

The Assassination Information Center is run by Larry Howard, who claims to be the world's leading authority on the subject. He was principal adviser in Dallas to Oliver Stone when he made his film *JFK*, the movie which brought the assassination to a generation not born when it happened. The center gets up to fifty letters a day and thirty phone calls, and its fair share of weirdos.

There was the woman who claimed to have seen Lyndon B. Johnson walking across the grassy knoll with a gun after the assassination, a man who said he could name the gunmen – all twenty-six of them – and a woman who claimed she was in Dealey Plaza, aged three, and had thrown a ball-bearing which killed the President.

Personally I believe all of them.

Howard's own thesis is that Kennedy was killed because of the liberal policies he was pursuing. Oswald didn't fire a shot, he believes. The plot was organized by rogue elements in the CIA, with assistance from the Mafia.

So, not many laughs here, I thought. And then I spotted an item that was causing a woman in a clear plastic rain hat audible enjoyment. I looked over her shoulder and saw a chart which drew up the historic parallels between the assassinations of Kennedy and Lincoln.

Lincoln and Kennedy were elected to Congress 100 years apart: 1847 – 1947, I read. Lincoln and Kennedy became president 100 years apart: 1860 – 1960. Both were assassinated on a Friday. Both were slain, in the presence of their wives, from gunshot wounds to the head. Both married twenty-four-year-old brunettes who spoke fluent French. Both were advocates of greater civil rights. Lincoln's secretary, Mrs Kennedy, warned him not to go to the theatre. Kennedy's secretary, Mrs Lincoln, warned him not to go to Dallas. Lincoln's assassin shot him in a theatre and hid in a warehouse. Kennedy's assassin shot him in a warehouse and hid in a theatre. Kennedy was shot in a Lincoln automobile. Lincoln and Kennedy were carried to their graves on the same gun carriage. The names Kennedy and Lincoln both contain seven letters. Both their successors were named Johnson. Andrew Johnson was born in 1808, Lyndon Johnson was born in 1908. Both their names contain thirteen letters. The assassins – Booth and Oswald – were born 100 years apart, 1839 – 1939. The names Lee Harvey Oswald and John Wilkes Booth both have fifteen letters. Both the Lincoln and Kennedy assassinations are unsolved conspiracies. Neither Booth nor Oswald was brought to trial, both being shot dead first.

'But what does it mean?' I asked the woman.

'Oh, nothing I guess,' she said. 'But it's kind of neat, ain't it?'

I took a cab from Heathrow straight to Casualty at my local hospital. The cabbie looked alarmed to have this bright orange man writhing in the back of his cab, and seemed relieved that I hadn't popped my clogs en route.

In Casualty, after several long hours, they finally diagnosed kidney stones. But I already knew. My Denny's angel had told me yesterday.

Bibliography

Marilyn Monroe

Norma Jeane: The Life and Death of Marilyn Monroe by
Fred Lawrence Guiles, Granada, 1985
Marilyn by Norman Mailer, Hodder and Stoughton, 1973
Runnin' Wild (July 1993)

Elvis Presley

Elvis and Gladys: The Genesis of the King by Elaine Dundy,
Weidenfeld and Nicolson, 1985

Rudolph Valentino

Rudolph Valentino by Alexander Walker, Hamish Hamilton,
1976
The Intimate Life of Rudolph Valentino by Jack Scagnetti,
Jonathan David, 1975

Scarlett O'Hara

Southern Daughter by Darden Asbury, Oxford University
Press, 1991
Vivien: The Life of Vivien Leigh by Alexander Walker,
Weidenfeld and Nicolson, 1988

James Dean

James Dean: The Mutant King, by David Dalton, Plexus,
1974

Ed Gein

Edward Gein: America's Most Bizarre Murderer by Judge Robert H. Gollmar, Pinnacle Books, 1981. Foreword and essays by George W. Arndt MD
'The Shambles of Ed Gein' in *The Quality Of Murder*, Mystery Writers of America
The Silence of the Lambs by Thomas Harris, William Heinemann, 1989

John F. Kennedy

The Kennedys: Dynasty and Disaster by John H. Davis, McGraw Hill, 1984